CAMBRIDGE LIBRARY COLLECTION

Books of enduring scholarly value

Literary Studies

This series provides a high-quality selection of early printings of literary works, textual editions, anthologies and literary criticism which are of lasting scholarly interest. Ranging from Old English to Shakespeare to early twentieth-century work from around the world, these books offer a valuable resource for scholars in reception history, textual editing, and literary studies.

Our Recent Actors

Love of the theatre began at an early age for John Westland Marston (1819–90), and developed into his life's work as a playwright, critic and literary figure of the Victorian era. He fell out of fashion and into poverty in the last years of his life, though Irving and other friends helped with a gala benefit performance of his most famous play. This two-volume work, published in 1888, is a tribute to the actors, plays and performances of his youth. Victorian dramatic works ranged through a variety of styles and genres, and Marston's recollections cover the wide area of theatrical culture in which he was involved. Volume 1 includes chapters on the actors Macready, Charles and Ellen Kean and the Kemble family. Combining professional knowledge, backstage anecdotes and accounts of the emotional impact of performances upon Marston himself, the work offers an insight into the growth and development of nineteenth-century theatre.

T0382215

Cambridge University Press has long been a pioneer in the reissuing of out-of-print titles from its own backlist, producing digital reprints of books that are still sought after by scholars and students but could not be reprinted economically using traditional technology. The Cambridge Library Collection extends this activity to a wider range of books which are still of importance to researchers and professionals, either for the source material they contain, or as landmarks in the history of their academic discipline.

Drawing from the world-renowned collections in the Cambridge University Library and other partner libraries, and guided by the advice of experts in each subject area, Cambridge University Press is using state-of-the-art scanning machines in its own Printing House to capture the content of each book selected for inclusion. The files are processed to give a consistently clear, crisp image, and the books finished to the high quality standard for which the Press is recognised around the world. The latest print-on-demand technology ensures that the books will remain available indefinitely, and that orders for single or multiple copies can quickly be supplied.

The Cambridge Library Collection brings back to life books of enduring scholarly value (including out-of-copyright works originally issued by other publishers) across a wide range of disciplines in the humanities and social sciences and in science and technology.

Our Recent Actors

Being Recollections Critical,
and, in Many Cases, Personal, of Late
Distinguished Performers of Both Sexes

VOLUME 1

WESTLAND MARSTON

CAMBRIDGE UNIVERSITY PRESS

Cambridge, New York, Melbourne, Madrid, Cape Town,
Singapore, São Paolo, Delhi, Mexico City

Published in the United States of America by Cambridge University Press, New York

www.cambridge.org
Information on this title: www.cambridge.org/9781108047661

© in this compilation Cambridge University Press 2012

This edition first published 1888
This digitally printed version 2012

ISBN 978-1-108-04766-1 Paperback

OUR RECENT ACTORS

BEING

RECOLLECTIONS

CRITICAL, AND, IN MANY CASES, PERSONAL,

OF LATE DISTINGUISHED PERFORMERS
OF BOTH SEXES.

*WITH SOME INCIDENTAL NOTICES OF
LIVING ACTORS.*

BY

WESTLAND MARSTON.

IN TWO VOLUMES.

VOL. I.

LONDON:

SAMPSON LOW, MARSTON, SEARLE & RIVINGTON,
LIMITED,
St. Dunstan's House,
FETTER LANE, FLEET STREET, E.C.
1888.

LONDON :
PRINTED BY WILLIAM CLOWES AND SONS, LIMITED,
STAMFORD STREET AND CHARING CROSS.

TO

JOSEPH KNIGHT, ESQ.,

OF LINCOLN'S INN, BARRISTER-AT-LAW.

———◦◆◦———

My dear Friend,

It may probably have occurred to you, as it has done
to myself, to glance in leisure moments at the dedications
which were published a century or two ago. I confess to
having read them with considerable amusement, and,
perhaps, with a slight feeling of contempt; for the poet's
praise of the patron was usually in such superlatives, that
he often evinced more imagination in his dedication than in
his poem. Were the patron a warrior, he was, at least, an
Achilles; were he a poet, one would think that Homer and
Shakspere ought to hold up his train; were he a legislator,
Solon or Lycurgus would be eclipsed; while, in the event
of the book being inscribed to a lady, the three Goddesses
who contended for the golden apple were at once super-
seded in their respective attributes by the modern divinity.
One naturally reproaches such clients, to use the old phrase,
with insincerity and servility.

And yet I have at length learned, from experience, some
toleration for them, for *you* have taught me that seeming
hyperbole may well consist with truth. Of the man whose
imaginative sympathy and refinement have not only endeared

him to some of our best poets, but made him a poet himself; of the critic whose rare discernment has been in nothing more conspicuous than in his quick detection of merit; of the friend who has rejoiced in the successes of others as if they had been his own, while their misfortunes have called forth his untiring devotion—" Victrix causa diis placuit, sed victa Catoni; "—of such a man, I draw a portrait which, though absolutely faithful, may be regarded by those who do not know him as purely ideal.

Accept from me these Recollections touching an art in which we are both deeply interested, and

Believe, dear Knight,

In the profound and grateful affection of

Yours always,

WESTLAND MARSTON.

PREFACE

IT has often been asserted that the mere glamour
of youth induces playgoers to prefer their early
favourites to the actors who succeed them,
though the latter may be of equal or even of
superior merit. Were such a statement absolutely true, the writer of these pages might have
an additional reason for distrusting his fallible
judgment, especially in the cases of those bygone
performers with whom he was acquainted. It
may, nevertheless, well be that the assertion in
question, if true at all, is chiefly true with
respect to that part of the public which has laid
aside theatrical interests with youth, and which,
on occasionally repairing to the theatre in later
days, brings with it a mind which has lost its
old ardour not only by time and disuse, but by
the grave pursuits and anxieties of mature years.
With those, however, whose sympathy with

dramatic art has not been interrupted, the case, it
may be hoped, is different. Long experience may
possibly, in their instances, have more than
counteracted early bias and even personal regard,
while a yet warmer interest than that of youth
in theatrical representations may have been
developed by habit and opportunities of comparison. In the list of these the author trusts
that he may be included. As a matter of fact,
it has happened to him, as to many old playgoers, to find, in numerous cases, the same enjoyment from the present race of actors as that
derived from their predecessors. In some few
cases the enjoyment has even been superior.
With the class of playgoers described, whatever
the correctness of their judgment, there is at least
a desire to judge impartially, and to estimate
each performer, in each part, according to his
individual merits. With these critics the unfor-
gotten power of Macready, in the play-scene in
"Hamlet," has not blinded them to the excellence
of Mr. Irving in the same scene; they who most
admired the former actor can admit that Salvini

surpassed him in Othello. The remembrance of the great Rachel has not prevented them from seeing in Ristori, Sarah Bernhardt, and Madame Modjeska, a tenderness in which she was often deficient. Helen Faucit, Ellen Tree, Charles Kemble, have not left us insensible to the claims of Mr. Hare, of the Bancrofts and the Kendals, of Miss Terry, Mrs. Bernard Beere, Miss Ada Cavendish, or Miss Amy Roselle. Recollections of Liston, Harley, Keeley, or Wrench, have not deprived the humours of Mr. Toole, Mr. John S. Clarke, or Mr. Thomas Thorne of their mirth-moving power; nor have the gallantry and ardour of Mr. James Anderson rendered us indifferent to the same fine qualities in Mr. Henry Neville.

The "Recollections," whether critical or personal, have chiefly reference to past actors. Sometimes, however, living performers have been commented on either when comparison between themselves and their predecessors seemed desirable, or when they have so long retired from the stage that their career is become part of its history, or where they have been particularly associated with some remarkable event—such, for instance, as Phelps's management of Sadler's Wells. Many names of contemporary actors are, however, omitted, which would have high claims to notice had the writer's main object been to treat of the existing Stage.

In some rare cases, when the press and general report have pronounced a performance strikingly representative of the actor, the writer has given a sketch of it in his own words, though he may not have seen it. Notices of this kind have been derived partly from consultation of journals of authority, partly from statements of friends —some of whom were critics of celebrity, and minute in their information. The sketches referred to are those of Mr. Charles Kemble in Mark Antony (" Julius Cæsar "); of Mr. W. Farren in Michael Perrin (" Secret Service "), and in Old Parr; of Mr. Phelps in Sir Pertinax MacSycophant; of Mr. Alfred Wigan in " Still Waters Run Deep;" of Mr. Charles Mathews as Sir Charles Coldstream in " Used Up ;" and the brief reference to Mr. Webster as Richard Pride.

CONTENTS.

VOL. I.

PREFACE . . . . v *[PAGE]*

CHAPTER I.

EARLY ACQUAINTANCE WITH LONDON THEATRES—DENVIL,
VANDENHOFF, AND OTHER ACTORS.

Coming to London—First visits to theatres—Sadlers'
Wells — Miss Macarthy — Mr. G. Almar — Mr.
Cobham—Mr. T. P. Cooke—Mr. T. Archer—
Anecdote of him and Macready—Covent Garden
—Manfred—Miss Ellen Tree—Mr. Denvil—Mr.
Vandenhoff—His chief performances—Anecdote
of him—Miss Vandenhoff 1

CHAPTER II.

MACREADY, AND OTHERS OF HIS CONTEMPORARIES.

Juvenile disappointments with regard to certain actors
—Causes of this—Mr. Samuel Butler and Mrs.
Lovell—Surrey Theatre under Davidge—Butler's
extreme tallness a disadvantage—Author first sees
Macready in "Macbeth" at Drury Lane—Effect
of his performance—His Hamlet—His fracas with
Bunn—His reference to it in conversation eight
years afterwards, and advice to the author—Macready in Lord Lytton's " Duchess de la Vallière,"
at Covent Garden—Helen Faucit—Macready as
Melantius in "The Bridal" — Adaptation by

PAGE

Knowles of "The Maid's Tragedy"—Detailed
criticism of Macready's acting in this play—Criticism of his Virginius—His lesseeship of Covent
Garden—Success of "Henry the Fifth" and "The
Tempest"—His Richelieu—Account of the first
night's performance—Note—Macready somewhat
dissatisfied—Mr. Edwin Booth's Richelieu—The
author's first play—Macready's acceptance of it
for Drury Lane, of which he was become lessee—
Visit to him at that theatre—First impression of
going behind the scenes—First interview with
Macready—His genial welcome — His personal
appearance and manner of speaking—Talk as to
my play and as to Miss Helen Faucit—As to his
own part in the piece, and his fear of being too old
to look it—His objection combated—Reference to
"The Lady of Lyons"—Its early want of attraction and subsequent success—Charm of Macready's
manner 25

CHAPTER III.

MACREADY—*Conclusion.*

Macready's friends and acquaintance—At dinner with
him—His guests—His first wife and his sister—
Table-talk—Browning's "Blot on the Scutcheon"
—Opera of "Acis and Galatea"—Its admirable
cast—Unprecedented beauty of its reproduction—
Scenery by Stanfield—Invention of a stage-sea
with motion and sound—Compliment paid to Mac-
ready by a lady on the production of the opera—
Pictures and picture-dealers—Pæstum and the
Romans—The poet Pope—Humorous remini-
scences—Anecdote of Porson—Macready a Liberal
in politics—His objection to the phrase, "lower
classes"—An evening reception at his house—
Singing of Herr Staudigl in "Acis and Galatea"—
Assembly of celebrated authors, artists, &c.—
Macready's irritability at rehearsals, &c.—Author's
impression that this was to a great extent assumed
—His King Lear—This, in the writer's judgment,

PAGE

his greatest Shaksperian performance—Detailed
account of it—Macready's motto, " Patience is
genius," examined—Unjust to his own spontaneity
—Walter Scott and Sheridan Knowles—Macready's disparagement of Garrick—His theory
that goodness was essential to genius—His Macbeth—Regarded by his friends as his *chef d'œuvre*
—Examination of his performance at length—Also
of his Hamlet—His Othello, Iago, Evelyn in
" Money "—His Benedick in " Much Ado "—His
great performance of Werner—Full account of it
—Summary of his various characters—His psychological insight and artistic power of expressing
emotion—His King John—His Shylock—Anecdote in note as to his revival of " King John " at
Drury Lane—His Gisippus—His Spinola in " Nina
Sforza "—His religious sentiment—The characters
peculiarly suited to him—His defects and peculiarities—Comparison of him with contemporary
actors—His intensity—In certain parts approaching Edmund Kean's—General estimate of his
genius—His death   60

CHAPTER IV.

MR. CHARLES KEMBLE.

A summer evening at the West End, in the season of
1835—Charles Kemble's Hamlet, at the Haymarket—Cast of the tragedy—Charles Kemble's
appearance and manner — Description of his
Hamlet—His return to the stage in 1840, by
command of Her Majesty—Account of his Mercutio in " Romeo and Juliet "—His readings at
Willis's Rooms, in 1844—Account of his Faulconbridge in " King John," and his readings of that
play generally—Presence of the Queen Dowager
—Personal acquaintance with Charles Kemble—
Various fireside readings—Shylock—Richard the
Third—His tragic recitations generally—Resolution not to attempt John Kemble's parts, with the
exception of Hamlet, till his brother retired—

PAGE

Contrast of Charles Kemble's style with that of
Macready, and (by report) of the elder Kean—
His private readings or recitations in comedy—
A gentleman of the old school in private—Dignity
of his manner and appearance—His conversation
generally serious, with occasional passages of
humour—Anecdote of his brother John—Dispute
as to the intelligence of a popular actor—A test-
prologue written for his recitation—The prologue
in question—Mr. Kemble's deafness and habit of
making his confidences aloud—Anecdotes illustra-
tive of this—His Epicurean tastes—Talk on the
drama—Suggestion of plots—A domestic story—
The reign of Henry the Second—Mr. David
Roberts, R.A.—Mexico and Montezuma—General
estimate of him as an actor—Leigh Hunt's testimony on his retirement—His minuteness of treatment often unfavourable to passion—Mrs. Siddons
on his Jaffier—General admiration of his Mark
Antony—John Oxenford on the consistency of his
characterization, instanced in Charles Surface—
Charles Kemble's death, at the age of seventy-nine   109

CHAPTER V.

MR. WILLIAM FARREN, THE ELDER.

Difficulty of replacing him in various characters—His
son heir to some of his traditions—Lord Ogleby
and Sir Peter Teazle belong to a relatively new era
in comedy—The man of fashion from the reign of
Charles the Second to that of George the Third—
Account of Farren's Sir Peter Teazle—A vein of
indulgent cynicism characteristic both of his Sir
Peter and his Lord Ogleby—Account of the latter—
His Malvolio—His Sir Anthony Absolute—Want
of robustness and heartiness— A painter of well-
bred people, with their vanities, and other foibles,
and redeeming qualities—Excellent in the pathos
attaching to mental or bodily infirmities—His best
known characters but few—His Bertrand in " The
Minister and the Mercer "—His Michael Perrin in

PAGE

" Secret Service," in 1834—The latter piece revived
at Covent Garden, in 1840—His Michael Perrin
described—His performance at the Olympic, under
Madame Vestris, in 1837 and 1838—His acting in
" Sons and Systems," and in "The Court of Old
Fritz"—His Old Parr at the Haymarket, in 1843
—His chief excellence in characters of mental or
bodily infirmity—A touch of the morbid necessary
to his pathos—His persuasion that he could act
tragedy—His attempt at Shylock—His fine discrimination as to expression in acting—Instance of
this—His personal appearance—His death   151

CHAPTER VI.

MR. AND MRS. KEAN.

The latter part of Charles Kean's career the most notable,
    though his reappearance in Hamlet, at Drury Lane,
    in 1838, a great success—Account of this per-
    formance—Charles Kean less successful in other
    Shaksperian characters—Imitations of his father
    adapted in 1838—Afterwards abandoned—Effect
    of this change—His Macbeth in 1849—His Romeo
    —His Richard the Third—This character ranked
    next to his Hamlet in Shaksperian plays—Reasons
    for his superiority in Hamlet—Personal acquain-
    tance with Mr. and Mrs. Charles Kean—Favourable
    first impressions of them—Their generous appre-
    ciation of dramatic work—They appear, in 1849,
    at the Haymarket, in the author's tragedy entitled
    " Strathmore "—Mr. Kean's performance in this
    play—Some difference of view between him and
    the author—Mr. and Mrs. Charles Kean at re-
    hearsal—Her solicitude for him—Their appearance
    in " The Wife's Secret "—Mr. George Lovell—
    Journey of the writer and a friend with Charles
    Kean to Brighton—A delicate discussion on the
    way with respect to Phelps and Sadler's Wells—
    Peace secured—An amicable dinner—Change in
    his style of acting soon after entering with Keeley
    on management of the Princess's Theatre, in 1850

—More original hitherto in comedy than tragedy
—His Master Ford—His Benedick—His Mephistopheles in " Faust and Marguerite "—The change
in his acting foreshadowed in his comedy—First
exemplified in serious drama in " The Templar,"
by Mr. Selous —His acting in " Anne Blake"
— He appears in " Louis the Eleventh," in
" The Corsican Brothers," and in " Pauline "—
He reads to the author various scenes from
" Louis the Eleventh," some time before its production—Great impression produced—A triumph
confidently predicted—Account of his performance — Rises to genius in this and other character parts—Account of his Louis the Eleventh
— This his greatest achievement — Mr. Henry
Irving in the same part—Charles Kean's visit to
Plessy-les-Tours—His Wolsey—His Richard the
Second—Spectacular and archæological revivals—
Danger of excess in these directions—Charles Kean
in private—His forgivable egoism—His *bonhomie,*
humour, love of fun, and winning avowal of his
weaknesses—His sly raillery of Mrs. Kean on her
susceptibility—Decline of taste for legitimacy—
A melancholy pledge—Quarrel with a dramatic
author—The alleged price of listening to a story—
Ex parte statement as to the way commissions
were obtained from him—Mrs. Kean's sympathy
with him—Hereditary genius—His father's fame,
in his opinion, detrimental to him—His strong
desire to find his opinions adopted and his side in
a quarrel espoused—This illustrated by his difference with Douglas Jerrold—Causes of this—Censure of Mrs. Kean's acting by a critic—Charles
Kean's strange method of resenting this, and annoyance with the author for disapproving of his
retaliation—His avowed objection to impartial criticism. The model of a theatrical notice—Hears
a detailed eulogy of his wife's acting in a particular play—Demands the speaker's opinion at equal
length on his own acting—Resents the notion that
a man ought not to be praised to his face—His expedient for meeting this objection—A last inter-

PAGE

view with him—A glimpse of him, during illness,
at Scarborough—His death—Brief summary of his
claims, professional and private   .   .   . 168

CHAPTER VII.

MRS. CHARLES KEAN.

Mrs. Charles Kean (then Ellen Tree) in "The Red
Mask," at Drury Lane, in 1834—Her acting in
"The Jewess," etc., in 1835—The original Clemanthe in Talfourd's "Ion," at Covent Garden—
She subsequently appears as Ion at the Haymarket
—Notice of her performance—Appears, in 1839,
at Covent Garden, under the management of Mr.
and Mrs. Charles Matthews, as the Countess in
Sheridan Knowles's "Love"—The run, then extraordinary, of that piece—Macready's statement
as to the then average attraction of legitimate
plays, and as to "The Lady of Lyons"—Miss
Ellen Tree's acting as the Countess—As Ginevra,
in Leigh Hunt's play, "The Legend of Florence,"
at Covent Garden, 1840—Leigh Hunt's tribute to
her—Appears, same year, in Knowles's "John of
Procida," at Covent Garden—In 1842 (then Mrs.
Charles Kean) appears at the Haymarket in
Knowles's "Rose of Arragon"—Her acting in the
two plays last named—Indifferent as Juliet and
Lady Macbeth—Description of her acting in the
latter—Her Gertrude in "Hamlet," Marthe in
"Louis the Eleventh," Katherine in "Strathmore," and Anne Blake in the play so called—
Brief summary—Personal appearance—Her death 216

CHAPTER VIII.

MR. BENJAMIN WEBSTER.

First acquaintance with Mr. Webster — "Borough
Politics"—His quarrel with Mr. and Mrs. Charles
Matthews—His habit of confiding differences to
others—Called a "good hater"— Certainly a

PAGE

staunch friend—Of a sensitive disposition—His
feeling of comradeship — His resentments not
lasting—His reported challenge to Macready—
His fidelity, as manager, to the interests of his
company — Interview with him — His personal
appearance and manner—An agreement concluded
—His bandinage—His frankness and promptness
in negotiations—His acting in a little comedy by
the writer—Width of his range—His desire to
extend it—I read to him some scenes of a poetic
drama of which I desire him to play the hero—
His pleasure at the proposal and his misgiving—
Reasons for it—Variety of his acting in dramas of
real life—Account of his acting in " The Roused
Lion "—Allusion to the excellence of Mrs. Keeley
in the same drama—His acting as Squire Verdon
in " Mind Your Own Business "—His nice balance
of various features of character—This exemplified
—His Richard Pride—His Graves in "Money,"
Triplet in " Masks and Faces "—Reuben Gwynne
in " The Round of Wrong "—His Tartuffe—Objec-
tions to that comedy—His Jesuit Priest in " Two
Loves and a Life "—His Robert Landry in " The
Dead Heart "—Mr. David Fisher in that drama—
Mr. Webster as Penn Holder in " One Touch of
Nature "—His faults—His Petrucchio—His Wild-
rake in " The Love Chase "—Dragging delivery in
his later years—His services as a manager—" The
Heart and the World "—Supper after a failure—
Dinner to Webster at Freemasons' Tavern—The
Shakspere Committee—Webster's institutions for
actors—His reception in Paris by Napoleon III.
—Mr. Robert Bell—Welcome to Keeley—Webster's
death—His reputation as an actor and in private . 233

CHAPTER IX.

MRS. GLOVER.

Mrs. Glover in early days had often appeared in tragedy
—Had performed Hamlet—First saw her as Gertrude, to Charles Kemble's Hamlet—Her eninence

PAGE

as an actress of comedy—Her truth to nature—
Her keen perception of characteristics, moderation,
and air of unconsciousness—These merits exemplified in her Mrs. Malaprop—Her performance of
the character compared with Mrs. Stirling's—Mrs.
Glover's Mrs. Candour—Her Nurse in "Romeo
and Juliet"—Her Widow Green in "The Love
Chase"—The original Lady Franklin in "Money"
—Her Miss Tucker in "Time Works Wonders"
She appears in a comedy called "The Maiden
Aunt," by R. B. Knowles—Acts in the writer's
comedy, "Borough Politics" — Account of her
performance—Meeting with her at rehearsal—An
argument with the author—Minuteness and fulness of her observation — Her sympathy with
authors—Thackeray's tribute to her acting—
Reported connection of her family with the famous
Betterton—Her death 260

CHAPTER X.

MRS. WARNER.

Mrs. Warner's rank as an actress—Performs both the
gentler and sterner characters in tragedy—At
Covent Garden and Drury Lane with Macready—
Had appeared, in 1836, as the heroine of Knowles's
"Daughter"—Her Joan of Arc, Lady Macbeth,
and Hermione—Her power in invective and in
irony — Her fine impersonations of Emilia in
"Othello," and of Evadne in "The Maid's Tragedy"
—Account of her acting in these characters—
Evadne her chief triumph—Enthusiastic praise of
it by Dickens—After separating from Phelps, Mrs.
Warner attempts, in 1847, to make the Marylebone
Theatre a Western Sadler's Wells—Eventual failure
of the scheme—During her management of the
Marylebone, Mrs. Warner appears as Hermione,
Julia, Lady Teazle, Mrs. Beverley, Mrs. Oakley,
and Lady Townley—Her want of flexibility in
comedy—Great merit, nevertheless, of her Mrs.
Oakley—The event of her first season at the

PAGE

Marylebone the magnificent and correct reproduction of Beaumont and Fletcher's " Scornful Lady "
—Remarks on this comedy—The character of the
heroine remarkably suited to her—Mrs. Warner
in private—First meeting with her at rehearsal at
Drury Lane, in 1842—Her acute and humorous
remarks on Macready's realistic getting up of
" The Patrician's Daughter "—Anecdote told by
her of impracticable stage effects—Her easy and
genial manners in private, for the exhibition of
which her stage characters gave few opportunities
—Her last illness and death   274

OUR RECENT ACTORS.

CHAPTER I.

EARLY ACQUAINTANCE WITH LONDON THEATRES—
DENVIL, VANDENHOFF, AND OTHER ACTORS.

Coming to London—First visits to theatres—Sadler's Wells—
Miss Macarthy—Mr. G. Almar—Mr. Cobham—Mr. T. P.
Cooke—Mr. T. Archer—Anecdote of him and Macready—
Covent Garden—Manfred—Miss Ellen Tree—Mr. Denvil
—Mr. Vandenhoff—His chief performances—Anecdote of
him—Miss Vandenhoff.

THIS book is, so far as it goes, an autobiography.
It is a narrative touching persons and things
seen by the writer, with the exception, in some
few cases, of matters which became known to
him on trustworthy authority. He has tried to
say as little about himself as consists with the
due setting of his various portraits. He has

not forgotten, however, how much in autobiography (witness the diaries of Pepys and Evelyn)
a touch of surrounding detail gives life to the
chief matter described. Thus in the notice of
Mr. Charles Kemble he has recalled the bright
summer weather, the brilliant whirl of London
in the height of the season, and the gay and
crowded thoroughfares of the West End through
which he made his way to the Haymarket. Such
details, moderately used, give reality to the
pictures they frame, and bring them down from
the abstract by relating them to particular times
and circumstances.

To speak in the first person, which, spite of
its necessary egotism, is the most convenient
form of narrative, I came from the Lincolnshire
seaport and market-town of Great Grimsby to
London in the year 1834, having at that time
attained my fifteenth year. It had been arranged
that I should be articled to my uncle, a solicitor,
who, with his partner, had offices near Gray's
Inn. The partner's house was my first abode,
and here I found—or perhaps I should say,

took—more liberty of action during my evenings than was quite suitable in the case of so mere a boy.

Two years previously, on my first visit to London, I had been arrested by the playbills of the great patent theatres and by the magical name—then still a sound of lingering greatness—of Edmund Kean. "Drury Lane!" "Covent Garden!" "Mr. Kean!" Strange how these words of romance had some way penetrated to me through the seclusion of a "serious" home in the country, where my excellent parents never mentioned the stage, except to warn me, or others, of its dangers and seductions.* Now that at a too early age I was, in many respects, my own master, and could indulge, if I chose, my longing to visit a theatre, I began to ask myself what there was in dramatic performances that should make them necessarily objectionable. I recalled my own annual displays when, as a lad of eleven or twelve, I had

---

* My father, who had seceded from the Church, was a dissenting minister.

appeared with my schoolmates at the Theatre Royal, Great Grimsby, in various dramatic characters, at one time sustaining on " breaking-up day " the part of Juba in " Cato," and another that of Electra in the tragedy of " Sophocles," and afterwards that of Miriam (the Christian convert) in Milman's " Jerusalem Delivered." I remembered, too, how much my father, a zealous lover of Sophocles, though a foe to the stage, had praised my rendering of Electra. Was it possible, I argued, that a mode of composition allowable and, indeed, admirable in Greek, should be censurable in English, or that dialogue which was innocent when read should become injurious when spoken in public, with dresses and scenery to assist the impression ? If the theatre might have its bad side, so also had literature, art, and even trade. If no judicious parent would put " Tom Jones " into a boy's hands, was that a reason for withholding the novels of Scott ? Must " Don Quixote " be forbidden because the word " fiction " applied also to " Gil Blas " ? With this kind of logic I extorted a reluctant permission from my conscience for an act which, if allowable in itself, was still one of grave disobedience towards affectionate parents. I can still recall the boyish sophistry which prompted me to choose Sadler's Wells Theatre for my first visit. It was a small theatre, and it was situated in a suburb—facts which, as they were likely to diminish my pleasure, seemed in the same degree to make my transgression a slight one. I might have gone to Covent Garden, I reasoned, and, at that renowned theatre, have revelled in the best acting of the day, whereas I self-denyingly contented myself with Sadler's Wells. On the night when I entered that (to me) enchanted palace, I found there a new opiate for my restless conscience. The title of the piece represented I quite forget, but its main situation is as fresh as ever in my memory. A girl, deeply attached to her betrothed, learns his life is at the mercy of a villain (of course, an aristocrat), whom she has inspired with a lawless passion. She implores his pity for her lover, only to find that the sacrifice of her

honour is the price of his ransom. I remember
how my heart came into my throat and the
tears into my eyes when the noble-minded girl,
striking an attitude of overwhelming dignity,
before which the wretch naturally abased himself,
spurned his offer, and committed her cause to
that Providence which, in the good, honest melodrama of that day, never delayed to vindicate
the trust reposed in it. What most comforted
me during the evening was the conviction that
my father, could he have seen the piece, would
heartily have applauded it and recanted at once
his unqualified enmity to the theatre. I fancied
how cordially, had he been behind the scenes,
he would have shaken hands with Miss Macarthy
(afterwards Mrs. R. Honner), who had no in-
considerable skill in painting the struggles of
virtuous heroines. I might certainly, however,
have trembled for the consequences had he
encountered a certain Mr. G. Almar, who, if my
memory serves me, personated the miscreant of
the drama.

I was curious enough, even on the first night

of attending a theatre, to ask myself why Mr. Almar made such incessant use of his arms. Now they were antithetically extended, the one skyward, the other earthward, like the sails of a windmill; now they were folded sternly across his bosom; now raised in denunciation; now clasped in entreaty, and considerately maintained in their positions long enough to impress the entire audience at leisure with the effect intended. I was critical enough to ask myself whether the more heroic attitudes of this gentleman would not have been heightened by the contrast of occasional repose, and whether there were, in his opinion, any fatal incompatibility between easy and natural gestures and effective acting. On quitting the theatre, my inquiring mind received some light upon these points, for in the window of a confectioner, who was also a theatrical printseller, my attention was arrested by coloured portraits of local, or other stage favourites, in their principal characters. Here figured " Mr. Cobham, as Richard the Third," with a frown to spread panic through the ranks of " Shallow

Richmond." Here was Mr. T. P. Cooke,* as
William in "Black-eyed Susan," in that renowned
hornpipe which illustrates William's happier
days, ere Susan and he had dreams of a court-
martial. And here figured my friend of "The
Wells," Mr. G. Almar, in various characters, in
all of which the use of his arms was so remarkable, that it might easily be inferred he acted
less for the sake of his general audience than
for that of the artist who depicted him, and who
probably would have thought little of an actor
who did not supply him with attitudes. I was
glad, moreover, to find from one of the prints
that Mr. Almar's arms were not always employed
to illustrate sinister characters, but that on occasions they could be virtuously engaged. In this
particular instance they represented the action of
the noble Rolla in "Pizarro," as he bears Cora's
rescued child triumphantly over the cataract.

---

   * I met one morning this famous nautical actor, during a call
on Mr. and Mrs. Charles Kean. Mr. T. P. Cooke's thorough
heartiness, "go," and physical activity, were the grounds of
his success. In private, his manners were frank and engaging.
He was greatly respected by the members of his profession.

On my second visit to Sadler's Wells, a drama taken from Scott's novel, "Rob Roy," was the leading piece. The part of the romantic cattle-lifter was performed by a Mr. Archer, whose demeanour in the part was singularly haughty. The erect carriage of his head, set upon a slender neck, his scornful look and folded arms, as he exclaimed to his captors, "Villains and slaves! you have not yet subdued Rob Roy!" were, to my young experience, in the last degree imposing. This gentleman, then fulfilling a star engagement at "The Wells," was, I believe, a well-known actor at the West End theatres. A droll anecdote, of which he was the hero, was told to me by the late Mr. Bayle Bernard. I give it pretty nearly in his own words, the humour of which seized on my memory.

On one of the performances of "Virginius," Archer had to sustain the part of the wicked Appius Claudius, to Macready's Virginius. In the last act, where Virginius, exclaiming—

> "And have I not a weapon to requite thee?
> Ah, here are ten!"

springs upon Appius and chokes him, Macready was so carried away by his own intensity, that his tight and prolonged grasp of Archer's throat had well-nigh converted the fictitious catastrophe into a real one. The half-suffocated representative of Appius bore his trial in meek silence on the night in question. Archer, however, who delighted in solemn fun, and who could humorously assume the grandiose language of the stage in private, had a lesson to read the tragedian. When Virginius was next performed, Macready, on entering the Green Room in the interval between the fourth and fifth acts, discovered that the throat of Archer was encased in a dark velvet collar, which, with its shining points, was a strange innovation on the costume of a Roman Decemvir. The Virginius of the night contemplated Appius awhile in gloomy silence, then slowly approached him. The shining points just mentioned were now seen to be small steel spikes, which protruded from the collar, and would infallibly give a rude reception to any hands which might grasp the neck it encased. As it was set down in Macready's part that he should perform this very operation, it is not surprising that he viewed the new feature of Mr. Archer's attire with decided disapproval. Breaking at length the absorbed silence which he usually maintained during his rare and brief visits to the Green Room, he addressed the object of his suspicion.

MACREADY. "Are you—are you—aware, Mr.—Mr. Archer, that that—that peculiar ornament round your neck is—is quite inappropriate to your character?"

ARCHER. "I admit it, sir; but the last time I had the honour of appearing with you in this rather unsympathetic part, you seized and held me with such violence that I hardly expected to act it again! Acting, after all, in my humble opinion, is but feigning. I am not a gladiator or a wrestler, sir, and I set some value upon my windpipe."

Macready, said my informant, for a moment put on an expression of lofty indignation, but,

whether from policy or from a sense of humour
(in which he was by no means deficient), he
quickly exchanged it for a look of amusement,
and, laying his hand familiarly on his brother
actor's shoulder—a rare condescension indeed,—
exclaimed—

"Archer, if my feelings carried me away
the other night, I apologize. I give you my
honour I will deal gently with you in future,
and that you will have no need of—of that
singular appendage by—by way of armour."

So the obnoxious collar was removed before a
summons came from the call-boy. Mr. Bernard
assured me that, in all essentials, this anecdote is
authentic.

Shortly after my second visit to Sadler's Wells,
I found myself a unit in a struggling crowd
at the pit entrance of Covent Garden. The
thought that I was soon to be within the walls
of so renowned a theatre had kept me in a
happy fever of wakefulness during the previous
night, and in the morning had possibly made
my perusal of "Chitty on Pleading," or the

last volume of " Reports on Equity," the most
barren of studies.

Covent Garden was at this time under the
management of Mr. Alfred Bunn.   He had
recently produced there Lord Byron's drama
of " Manfred," the dramatic picture in this case
having been put upon the stage less for its own
sake than for that of its gorgeous spectacular
frame.   Some histrionic ability had, however,
been enlisted for the piece.   Miss Ellen Tree
(whom I then saw for the first time) declaimed
the lines allotted to the Witch of the Alps—
lines which are not only few, but almost devoid
of dramatic force, serving only to draw out
Manfred's long and gloomy retrospect.   Nevertheless, in her appearance, as she stood within
the arch of a rainbow—in her garments, which
seemed woven of aerial colours touched by the
sun—and in her voice, the tones of which, though
sweet, were remote and passionless—she realized
all the weird charm of a genius of lake and
mountain.   There was something glacial in her
unsubstantial loveliness, something that belonged

to the forms of sleep rather than those of common day. Well, therefore, did Byron's sister write of this performance soon after the production of Manfred, "Miss Ellen Tree's Witch of the Alps I shall dream of."

The haughty and mysterious hero of the drama was represented by Mr. Denvil, who had performed with fair success the characters of Shylock and of Richard the Third. The new tragedian, though he subsequently failed in "Othello," had some measure of poetic feeling, and considerable power of facial expression. General praise was accorded to his Manfred. Boy though I was when I saw him in this part, I still remember his pale, almost spectral face, thrown out by his dark garb, and a haughty isolation and melancholy in tone, look, and gesture that well conveyed the mingled pride and remorse of one who, though racked by the sense of a hidden crime, has won commerce with supernatural beings. Very impressive was his delivery of the passage in which he recalls Astarte and her fate, nor less so the look of self-recoil which accompanied its close—

" She was like me in lineaments—her eyes,
  Her hair, her features, all, to the very tone
  Even of her voice, they said were like to mine ;
  But soften'd all, and temper'd into beauty :
  She had the same lone thoughts and wanderings,
  The quest of hidden knowledge, and a mind
  To comprehend the universe : nor these
  Alone, but with them gentler powers than mine,
  Pity, and smiles, and tears—which I had not ;
  And tenderness—but that I had for her ;
  Humility—and that I never had.
  Her faults were mine—her virtues were her own—
  I loved her and destroy'd her !
        Witch.   With thy hand ?
        Man. Not with my hand, but heart—which broke
            her heart ;—
  It gazed on mine, and wither'd."

The words in italics were given with an
intensity of horror and remorse that no actor
could well have surpassed. The judgment of a
lad of fifteen on this point may not be worth
much; but I find that the effect produced by
Denvil on myself was shared even by some
of those critics whose condemnation of his
subsequent performance of Othello was most
unsparing. Why an actor should be fairly
successful in Richard the Third and Shylock,
really fine in Manfred, and yet fail totally in

Othello, is not at once obvious. From the attacks of his critics, however, upon this last personation, the actor never recovered. A few years afterwards I saw him at one of the minor theatres as the hero of a melodrama. Possibly from a belief that the want of physical force was the cause of his previous defeat, Denvil had now so exclusively cultivated this quality that his acting had degenerated into the worst style of provincial rant. Of the ease, refinement, and poetic appreciation and quick insight into character and motive which he had at times exhibited, there was not a trace. Distorted features, violence of gesture, and strain of lung were all the resources left to him. Ere long he seems to have been quite forgotten by the public. It is said that he ultimately became check-taker at one of the minor theatres, and died in obscurity, in 1866. This story of self-realized oblivion on the part of an aspirant, who at the outset displayed some fine qualities of his art and gained some distinction, is, surely, deeply pathetic.

My visits to the theatre now became frequent.
I have a dim but pleasing recollection at this
time of "Man—Fred" (a capital burlesque of
"Manfred"), at the Strand Theatre, in which a
comedian named Mitchell performed the principal
character. He had a feeling of genuine humour,
which restrained him from undue exaggeration
in the part, while he showed a droll likeness to
the moods of his tragic original. When the
curtain rose, and Mitchell—I think, as a working
bricklayer—inspected with gloomy dejection an
empty quart measure, there was in his first
utterance—

> "The jug must be replenished; but even then
> It will not hold so much as I could drink;"

a deep, fixed, self-absorbed despondency, which
recalled, with delightful absurdity, Denvil's tones
as Lord Byron's hero—

> "The lamp must be replenished; but even then
> It will not burn so long as I must watch."

I saw and relished Mitchell in one or two
other comic characters, but soon lost sight of
him. It is on record that he achieved a marked

success at the St. James's Theatre, in 1836, in
a serious character, as the hero of a piece called
"The Medicant." I have an impression it was
shortly after this performance that he went to
America, where he died, at the age of fifty-seven,
in 1856.

About this time, too, I have recollections of
Mrs. Waylett as Apollo in "Midas." She had
a charming voice, an arch, bright expression, and
was not only a good vocalist, but fairly effective
in comedietta and farce. In these happy days
of youth I paid my first visit to the Olympic
Theatre, of which an account will be given in the
chapter on Madame Vestris. Ere long I found
myself within the walls of the Adelphi. There
I remember seeing Mrs. Honey in some farcical
piece, and Mr. John Reeve as Cupid. The lady's
one qualification for the part seemed to be a
pretty but already worn face, and a coquettish
simper; while the obesity of Mr. Reeve was the
chief point of humour in his assumption of Cupid.
I had previously seen him at the Queen's Theatre,
in Tottenham Street, in "Catching an Heiress,"

as an ostler who absurdly counterfeits a German
baron.   This performance, again, gave me no
particular idea of Reeve's humour.   The part
would have been droll in any hands if the
audience, as at " The Queen's," could once have
tolerated its extravagance.   I record, however,
impressions which may have been ill-founded.
My judgment was necessarily immature, and it
is not to be denied that both Reeve and Mrs.
Honey—the former especially—had a large circle
of admirers.   At the Adelphi, also, I first saw
Mr. O. Smith, celebrated for his delineations in
melodrama, both of villains and of supernatural
agents.   That he could be very thorough in such
personations, suggesting at times by his voice,
expression, and make-up unfathomable wickedness ; and again, that he could freeze the spectator
with his weird appearance and action in appari-
tions from another world, I can still recall.   He
was, in a word, the nightmare of the stage.   I saw
him seldom, however, and retain no clear remembrance of any of his particular characters.   A far
higher impression, though less distinct than I

could wish, is that of Mrs. Yates, wife of one of
the lessees. There flits before me the figure of
a slender, elegant woman, with a low, expressive
voice, capable of very subtle inflections. This
actress struck me as being eminently gifted with
quiet strength. Her power of this kind in sarcasm,
bitterness, or intense grief, was truly remarkable.
In the expression of these emotions she did not
seem to be acting; she spoke as a lady might
have spoken in a drawing-room, and moved you
without a trace of effort. A scene at a masked
ball, to which she tracked her faithless husband
and his mistress, stands out still in my recollection, though I have forgotten the details of that
particular scene; and, young though I was, I felt
how widely Mrs. Yates's suggestive acting, in
which feeling and intellect happily blended,
separated her from the many actresses who
mistake restlessness for animation, and violence
for power.

On the revival of "Othello" at Covent Garden,
for Denvil, the part of Iago was performed by the
elder Vandenhoff. It was in this character that

I first saw him; and, both from the testimony
of criticism at the time, and from my own impressions, I could scarcely have seen him to better
advantage.   He assumed a mask of impulsive
light-heartedness and *bonhomie*, a good-natured
pliancy which made him everywhere *bon camarade*.
There was at times even a sort of detestable gaiety
in his soliloquies and asides, as if the cleverness
of his wickedness and the follies of mankind
diverted him, and made it half a pastime to work
out his malignity.   I am by no means asserting
that this is the highest conception of Iago that
could have been formed, but it was original and
dashing; there was Italian subtlety in it, and
it gave great scope for the execution of Iago's
villainous designs.   The impulsiveness he so well
feigned in this part was a contrast to his usual
style of acting, which was elaborate and somewhat
heavy.   He had, however, great dignity, a powerful
and melodious voice, and his means of expression
had often been so happily thought out that, in
such characters as Coriolanus, Creon, in the
memorable English reproduction of Antigone, and

Adrastus in Talfourd's "Ion," his acting was finished and impressive. Pathos could by no means be called his strong point; yet sometimes his pathetic bursts (as in the case of Adrastus) were very telling, partly from their contrast with the general self-repression and dignity of his manner. He may be said to be the last prominent tragedian of the Kemble school, having a good deal of the stately carriage and bold outline of his predecessors, without, I suspect, quite the same tenacity of feeling and minuteness of suggestion which distinguished them. In his last days his acting became over-deliberate and tedious. In his prime, however, he was always more than respectable. Neither his Macbeth nor his Othello (which latter I saw him perform to Macready's Iago) were to be greatly praised for intensity of passion or for the light shed upon internal conflicts; yet his power of facial expression, his excellent elocution, largeness of style, and fine bearing, carried him successfully through.

I met Mr. Vandenhoff several times in society. He was agreeable, well-bred, and more addicted

to humour than could have been inferred from
any of his stage characters except Iago. An
amusing peculiarity of his may here be noted.
He had so great an antipathy to the "harmless,
necessary cat" that the presence of that animal
in the room was a trial beyond his endurance.
A friend of mine, whenever Mr. Vandenhoff was
expected, was accustomed to take the strictest
precautions that pussy might neither be found
coiled in comfort before a fire, nor flitting along
hall or staircase when her visitor ascended. On
one occasion, when he chanced to be her guest,
the ingenious animal contrived to defeat all the
means used for its exclusion, and entered the
drawing-room with the usual complacent cry of
a feline pet. A shriek at once gave vent to the
panic of the dismayed tragedian, who could
scarcely have been more appalled by the apparition of Banquo's ghost than by that of this
domestic favourite.

Miss Vandenhoff, the actor's daughter, though
her appearances on the stage were not frequent,
was an actress of considerable merit. She was

the original Parthenia in "Ingomar," and the original Margaret Aylmer in "Love's Sacrifice." Her performance of Antigone—the character in which Lady Martin (Miss Helen Faucit) won so much celebrity—was deservedly praised for its classic simplicity, its grace, and pathos. She had, too, an agreeable voice, and many passages of the tragedy were charmingly intoned. Miss Vandenhoff was herself the author of a drama, the heroine of which she performed at the Haymarket Theatre. It contained some poetic and telling lines. I recall one from the lips of a blind girl, when suffering from some cruel injustice—

"Only by tears I know that I have eyes."

Miss Vandenhoff died in 1860, at the age of forty-two; her father at that of seventy-one, in the following year.

These preliminary recollections bring me almost to the time when I first saw Macready.

CHAPTER II.

MACREADY, AND OTHERS OF HIS CONTEMPORARIES.

Juvenile disappointments with regard to certain actors—Causes
of this—Mr. Samuel Butler and Mrs. Lovell—Surrey
Theatre under Davidge—Butler's extreme tallness a dis-
advantage—Author first sees Macready in "Macbeth" at
Drury Lane—Effect of his performance—His Hamlet—
His fracas with Bunn—His reference to it in conversation
eight years afterwards, and advice to the author—Macready
in Lord Lytton's "Duchess de la Vallière," at Covent
Garden—Helen Faucit—Macready as Melantius in "The
Bridal"—Adaptation by Knowles of "The Maid's Tragedy"
—Detailed criticism of Macready's acting in this play—
Criticism of his Virginius—His lesseeship of Covent
Garden—Success of "Henry the Fifth" and "The
Tempest"—His Richelieu—Account of the first night's
performance—Note — Macready somewhat dissatisfied—
Mr. Edwin Booth's Richelieu—The author's first play—
Macready's acceptance of it for Drury Lane, of which he
was become lessee—Visit to him at that theatre—First
impression of going behind the scenes—First interview
with Macready—His genial welcome—His personal appearance and manner of speaking—Talk as to my play
and as to Miss Helen Faucit—As to his own part in the
piece, and his fear of being too old to look it—His objection combated—Reference to the "Lady of Lyons"—Its
early want of attraction and subsequent success—Charm of
Macready's manner.

A BOY'S ideal in art is not always easy to satisfy

—partly, perhaps, because he has a sharp appetite for the wonderful; partly because he is, to a great extent, unacquainted with the subtler and profounder emotions, and the symbols which represent them. Much that is really significant may have no meaning for him; reticence may be mistaken for tameness, and noisy excitement for feeling. However this may be, I had vaguely figured to myself more intensity and grandeur in tragic passion than I met with in the first year of my theatrical experience, except in the performances of Mr. Samuel Butler and Mrs. Lovell, formerly Miss Lacy, of Covent Garden. These performers occasionally played as "stars" at the Surrey Theatre, then under the management of that seasoned comedian of the old school, Mr. Davidge. Both of them were thoroughly in earnest, well trained in their art, and of commanding presence. The extreme height of Mr. Butler, indeed, was a disadvantage to him in a small theatre. In the capacious "Surrey," however, his uncommon stature was less perceptible. Like his fair associate, he was a good elocutionist, and, like her, he had the excellent quality of abandoning himself to passion without self-criticism. He never seemed to ask himself, as I have known actors of great intelligence do, "Shall I seem stagy if I adopt this movement? If I give passion full play here, shall I be accused of rant?" but, being already a proficient in the technical resources of his art, he trusted himself in good faith to the leading impulses of the character. I do not think he was given to rant. He occasionally exploded in sudden, vehement bursts, but they had the effect of being spontaneous—the outcome of passion accumulated and repressed. In the crises of feeling you saw, in him, that passion, though sometimes intensely hushed in white heat, darts forth at others in fiery tongues and roars—I do not care to use a weaker phrase —in its ascent. He was gifted, moreover, with a powerful voice, and had no need to hide the defects of a feeble physique by feigning that mysterious self-control which has since been called "repressed force." I saw little of Butler after the time I now write of, but enough to

confirm my first impressions of him. In Shylock
I was more carried away by him, so genuine was
his passion, than by any other actor I have seen
in the part. I will not undertake to say that his
interpretations were as profound as they were
undoubtedly vivid. I do know, however, that he
was "terribly in earnest," and that he had the
power of rousing masses to enthusiasm. His
excessive height, as has been said, was a great
disadvantage, and stood in the way of his being
fully appreciated. Finally, like most tragic actors
of his time, he was overshadowed by Macready;
but whether I owe the taste to Butler or to
nature, not, I hope, being insensible to higher
merits, I have never lost my liking for a good
physique, and, in many characters, for a good
display of it—in Othello, for instance, where
passion or intellect tell all the more if the actor
have also lungs. Mr. Butler died in 1845, at the
age of forty-eight; Mrs. Lovell, at that of seventy-
three, in 1877.

It was in 1835 that I first saw William
Charles Macready. The play was " Macbeth," the

theatre Drury Lane. This actor, always prominent from his first appearance in London, had,
since the death of Edmund Kean, gradually
won his way to the tragic throne.

The expectations which I had indulged as to
the first actor of his day must have been un-
reasonably high.   I remember comparing him
with my favourite, Butler, much to the advantage
of the latter. What, however, as a boy, in the
pit of Drury Lane, I missed in his Macbeth,
I still to some extent missed when, many years
later, I saw him take his final leave of the
public in the same character and at the same
house. Of his Macbeth, however, as of his other
characters, I shall speak afterwards in detail.
On my first acquaintance with it, spite of its
many excellences, I was disappointed in every
act except the last, in which the immense energy
and striking contrasts of his acting roused my
fervent admiration. The only other displays
by which the actor had greatly impressed his
precocious critic were his lost abstraction after
the temptation of the witches in the first act,

and his harrowing remorse after Duncan's murder, when dragged from the stage by Lady Macbeth, in the second act.

Hamlet was the next of his representations at which I "assisted." In this part his passionate and powerful acting absorbed and delighted me. It had the free impulse and the sense of the supernatural which I missed in much of his Macbeth.

It was soon after this performance that Macready, under considerable provocation, committed an assault upon Bunn, the Drury Lane manager. He was immediately engaged for Covent Garden, where, on his first appearance, the curious spectacle was exhibited of the public applauding an actor for conduct which he felt and confessed to be most blameworthy. British audiences are for the most part disposed to fairness as well as generosity. However, at times they allow themselves to become blind partizans, and to espouse (as they did in this case) a side enthusiastically for the sake of a favourite, rather than for that of justice. It is possibly a luxury to constitute themselves a jury, while dispensing with the judge's charge. Bunn's conduct in calling upon Macready to perform maimed characters was, no doubt, annoying, but he was legally within his rights, which the tragedian could scarcely say of his retaliation. I allude to this well-known quarrel chiefly for the sake of reporting Macready's own words to me upon the subject. Conversing with him in 1843, I happened to express some juvenile resentment at an attack made upon my first play by one who had previously been lavish in praise of it. Though I had possibly expressed myself warmly, to proceed against my assailant, "*par voie de fait*" had certainly not entered my mind. I was therefore not a little surprised to find myself suspected by my collocutor of pugilistic intentions. "Pass it over, pass it over, for Heaven's sake!" he exclaimed. "Contempt—quiet contempt—that's the proper answer. I have never forgotten," he continued, deepening his tone, "how frightfully I let myself be carried away in the case of that pitiful man,

Bunn. Though his behaviour to me was atrocious, in what I did I lost so far the right to self-respect. I have never forgiven myself for my violence. Always govern your temper, my young friend," he concluded, passing, with one of those transitions which use had made second nature to him, from a tone of agitation and excitement to one of calmness and paternal benignity.

I did not see the representation of Lord Lytton's play, "The Duchess de la Vallière," which was performed, under Mr. Osbaldiston's management, at Covent Garden. Though the piece was a failure on the stage, the general testimony was that Macready and Helen Faucit had seldom played with more splendid effect than in Bragelone and the Duchess.

Amongst the greatest impersonations of the former, out of Shakspere, was his Melantius in "The Bridal," an adaptation by Sheridan Knowles of "The Maid's Tragedy" of Beaumont and Fletcher. This work was produced, under Macready's auspices, at the Haymarket, which had recently passed under the control of Mr. Webster.

"The Bridal" was a great success. It increased my sense of Macready's genius, particularly of the finely harmonious variety of his method, which relieved and threw out the different aspects of his characters. His Virginius was scarcely finer than his Melantius, while in Evadne Mrs. Warner reached the summit of her power. The brave, loyal soldier, free and martial in his bearing, sincere almost to bluntness, seized the audience at once. Friendship, which Elizabeth's writers almost deify, glowed in Macready's bearing towards Amintor, with a generous and tender ardour which love itself could scarcely have surpassed. In our more worldly days, when the relations between men so seldom ripen beyond liking and good fellowship, the sympathizing devotion which set life and honour at a friend's disposal seems often mere extravagance. The old knightly sentiment, however, kindled into a blaze at Macready's contagious fire when he exclaimed—

> "The name of friend is more than family
> Or all the world beside!"

In the grand scene—one of the most passionate in English drama—in the fourth act, where Melantius forces Evadne to confession, it is hard to conceive that even Betterton, so famous in the part, could have been greater than the modern actor. There was at first a grim, sardonic air about him, suggesting a terrible mirth, in the way that lightning mocks daylight, that was terribly ominous of the coming outbreak; there was a suppressed passion, a boding calm, that held the listener in awe and apprehension, till at last the pent-up rage crashed out with such vehemence, it seemed as if nothing in its path could live.

In the adaptation of "The Maid's Tragedy" by Knowles, is a passage which, after careful search, I have not found in the original. It served to bring out with admirable effect one of Macready's colloquial and natural touches. The loyal Melantius, who has been secretly traduced to the King by one of his creatures, demands the name of his accuser. This is still withheld, when a dispute arises on some point of fact as to which one of the King's train persistently contradicts Melantius. This man's zeal betrays him as the author of the slander.

" Oh, then, it came from *him !* "

exclaims Melantius. Macready's quiet manner of delivering these words to the King, without turning to confront his accuser, whom he indicated behind him by a slight movement of the finger, expressed such superb contempt that the house rang with applause.

No feature of this actor was more specially his own than the sudden, yet natural, infusion into his more heroic vein of some homely touch of truth which gave reality to the scene—an achievement in his own art to which great poets have furnished abundant parallels in theirs, from Homer to Tennyson and Browning. Take a few examples from Macready's performance in Knowles's "Virginius;" first, the father's affectionate raillery of Virginia in the opening act, when he discovers that, in painting Achilles, she has unwittingly given him the features of her lover—

> "I've seen this face; tut, tut, I know it
> As well as I do my own; but can't bethink me
> Whose face it is."

Or, again, his impatient indulgence when Virginia clings round the neck of her betrothed, who is about to start with Virginius for the camp—

> "I swear a battle might be lost and won
> In half the time; now, once for all, farewell!"

Here is an instance of a graver kind. The free birth of Virginia has been impeached, and she is likely to be seized as a slave by the pander to Appius. In the midst of his rage at the infamous accusation, Virginius is struck by an expression on the face of his daughter—

> "I never saw you look so like your mother,
> In all my life."

Here Macready's transition from overmastering wrath to tenderness was made with such nature and force of contrast, that many of the audience wept. Knowles gave his exponent numerous chances for such colloquial touches. With this dramatist, indeed, they not only relieved a loftier style, but were often substituted for it.

One or two of the tragedian's revivals at Covent Garden I unfortunately missed. By all reports, not to see him in "Henry the Fifth," was to miss a quite distinct phase of his power. This privation I had somehow incurred, both with relation to the play last mentioned and to "The Tempest," the mere pictorial and stage arrangements of which seem to have been so beautiful and suggestive, as to set one of Shakspere's most spiritually poetic dramas in a frame of material poetry. Of one Covent Garden production, however, ever afterwards closely connected with his reputation, I have still most vivid remembrance.

In March, 1839, I fought my way with another young enthusiast to the pit door of old Covent Garden, on the first night of Bulwer's "Richelieu." What a human sea it was, and how lit up by expectation, that surged and roared for two hours against that grim, all-ignoring barrier! But its stubborn resistance, and the dense pressure which, at last, almost wedged out the breath of every unit in the crowd, gave an almost stern delight,

a zest of contest for a prize, of which the lounger
into a reserved box or seat has no conception.
The interest connected with a new play was
increased by the fact that Bulwer was the
author, for with us young critics his epigrams,
his rhetorical flashes, and, let it be said, a vein
of aspiration and generous feeling, rarely absent
from his later works, had made him a favourite.
We had an impression, moreover, that he was
hardly dealt with by a portion of the press, on
account of his politics. The future Lord Lytton
of Lord Derby's Government was at that time
a Liberal.

To return to " Richelieu," in which Macready
was perfection. I think I shall probably best
help my readers, not only to form an estimate
of his excellence in that play, but to gain a
general insight into his mind and method, if I
try to live over with them my old impressions
on the eventful first night of " Richelieu," from
the rise to the fall of the curtain. This method
of criticism is far too elaborate to be generally
employed, but for once I will have recourse to

it, and fancy that I am still fresh from the scene,
while describing to the listener an event nearly
fifty years old.

Suppose, then, the thronged house hushed, the
curtain raised, the gay scene of the conspirators
and gamesters going forward beneath the roof of
Marion de L'Orme. Even amidst the interest
of this opening scene, the thought of the house
escapes to Macready. Will he be discovered
with all the insignia of his rank and power?
Will he be closeted with Louis, or giving audience
to a spy? Will his manner have the pride of
the churchman, or the smoothness of the diplomatist? The first scene is over, and we have
our answer.

Macready, as the Cardinal, enters, followed by
the Capuchin Joseph, and the coming revelation
—signal, and in some respects new—of the actor's
powers, is at once foreshadowed by his appearance. How full of individuality are the whitening
hair, the face sharpened to the utmost expression
of subtlety and keenness, the gait somewhat loose
with age, but now quick and impulsive, now

slow or suddenly arrested, which seems to give a rhythm to the workings of his brain—to his swift, contemptuous penetration of the schemes against him, on the one hand, or, on the other, to his suspense, his caution, or his rapid decision. Soon followed one of those "ultra-collo-quialisms" which, when first reading the play, he had thought incompatible with Richelieu's dignity, but which, with the dry, caustic humour he gave them, were not only very telling, but seemed natural reliefs to the strained mind of the statesman. "Orleans heads the traitors," says Father Joseph; "A very wooden head, then!" exclaims Richelieu; and, though the sarcasm was threadbare, it had all the force of novelty and wit. Examples of the actor's unrivalled power in familiar touches abounded through the performance. His manner of exposing the strategy of Baradas to De Mauprat blended with contempt an easy penetration, an amused superiority, which was quite irresistible—

"Where was thy wit, man? Why, these schemes are glass;
 The very sun shines through them!"

Early in the play were encountered some of those dazzling, but rather forced metaphors, which the author's better judgment afterwards cancelled. Amongst these, however, was one which, as Macready gave it, drew great applause—

> " From rank showers of blood
> And the red light of blazing roofs you build
> The rainbow, Glory, and to shuddering Conscience
> Cry—Lo the Bridge to Heaven ! "

Soon after this example of poetic pyrotechnics, Richelieu charges De Mauprat with fraud. The indignant young man advances upon his accuser with an air and tone of menace when, it will be remembered, Huguet, one of Richelieu's guard, who waits armed behind a screen to intercept any possible violence to the Cardinal, raises his carbine to fire. Richelieu, with a wave of his hand, exclaims—

> " Not so quick, friend Huguet ;
> The Sieur de Mauprat is a patient man,
> And he can wait."

The dry, parenthetical utterance of these words, with the careless accompanying gesture, had in them the secret of a terrible humour and the proud assurance of a " charmed life " that no

succeeding impersonator of Richelieu has discovered. The whole of this first act is rich in
those contrasts of feeling and character in which
Macready delighted. The fervour with which,
after finding De Mauprat worthy of his confidence,
he asserts the justice of his rule, had in it all the
passionate earnestness and dignity of a man who,
long scornfully silent under misconception and
calumny, at last relieves his heart and vindicates
himself to an honourable judge. Soon follow the
lines in which, under pretence of dismissing De
Mauprat to death, he causes him to be conducted
to the presence of the woman for whose sake
he has braved it, this act, of course, implying
Richelieu's consent to their union. "Huguet,"
says he,

> " To the tapestry chamber
> Conduct your prisoner. (*To De Mauprat*) You will there
>   behold
> Your executioner. Your doom be private,
> And Heaven have mercy on you."

The rapidity and sternness with which these
lines were pronounced, as if only by hurry and
a forced overdoing of severity he could prevent

himself from giving way to the benevolent enjoyment of his device, showed one of the actor's
characteristic merits—his just perception of the
right note of feeling even to a semi-tone. The
look of sly and eager anticipation with which he
followed De Mauprat, as he retired, had in it
all the *bonhomie* which Bulwer,* rather than
history, ascribes to the Cardinal, and the zest
with which the sceptical mind of a diplomatist
may for once taste pure pleasure in bestowing it.

In the second act, the contrast between
Richelieu's usual scornful levity in dismissing the
schemes of his enemies, and the composed but
grave attention which denotes real peril, was
strikingly marked. With rapid step and hands
carelessly knotted behind him, he had paced to
and fro, listening to Father Joseph's rumours of
plots, either with incredulity or with smiling

* Having instinctively written the name by which the late
Lord Lytton was best known to his contemporaries, I let it
stand for the sake of remarking that, long after the celebrated
author had assumed the surname of Lytton, many of his
literary friends persisted in addressing him by that of Bulwer.
Their reluctance to forego the appellation under which he
had won so much distinction was a delicate tribute which
he doubtless appreciated.

confidence in his power to baffle them.　But
when Marion de L'Orme entered with news of
the conspiracy headed by Orleans, every trace of
caustic mirth or easy, exulting contempt at once
disappeared.　Of course, all actors would at this
point have made a transition of manner ; few,
indeed, would have made it with Macready's
arresting effect.　He questioned Marion in tones
the lowness of which expressed the intensity of
his interest.　His trust in his own resources was
still unshaken, but he felt that they might now
be taxed to the utmost.　The breathless audience
listened to the words, " Now there is danger," as
if each man had his personal stake in the crisis.
It was felt that if Richelieu could apprehend
danger, there must be danger indeed.　The tone
of gay flattery to Marion de L'Orme at that
moment of peril—

> "What an eye you have,
> And what a smile, child, . . . 'tis well I'm old,"

and the ringing exhortation to the page François,
when sent on his critical mission—" Never say
fail again ; that's my young hero ! " — were

brilliant examples of the actor's variety and
quick self-adaptation to his instruments. The
fascination which illustrious old age has for the
young and aspiring could never have been better
justified than by Macready's cheery laugh and
the look, full of kind encouragement, with which
he uttered these words to the page. I have
before me a copy of "Richelieu," marked from
the tragedian's acting copy of 1843 (four years
after the production of the play), in which the
compliment to Marion de L'Orme is cut out—
a mistake, I think, for his delivery of it was
certainly one of the brilliant facets which his
genius exhibited in this manifold character.

So full of fine variety was his delineation at
the close of this second act, as almost to atone
for its want of incident. His momentary distrust
of Huguet, as he noted "he bowed too low"
(some Richelieus have so over-emphasized this
trait of minute observation, that they should, to
be consistent, have discharged the guardsman on
the spot); his brief lapse into melancholy, as he
reflects on the snares that beset his bed and board,

and his friendlessness at the height of power;
his proud rally from these thoughts to faith in
the indomitable heart of Armand Richelieu, and
the quaint *bonhomie,* strangely compounded of
archness, good-feeling, and dissimulation, with
which he addresses Joseph,—all received their
just proportion. Each trait harmonized with,
and flowed into its fellow. There was no hard
line to divide, or even to distinguish, diplomacy
from sentiment or sentiment from humour, but
a living man in whom all these qualities naturally
blended.

The third act gave scope for the excellences
already noted, and with yet higher development.
The Richelieu who awaited, with breathless
eagerness, from François the proofs that should
convict Baradas; the Richelieu who, minutely
observant, even in his excitement, could pause to
note the small number of the conspirators—who,
learning that the despatch which would have
secured his triumph had been wrested from
François, one moment sternly warned him to see
his face no more till he had regained it, and

the next, relented into smiling encouragement—
" Away ! Nay, cheer thee ; thou hast not failed
yet; there's no such word as fail!"—was, in
these various aspects, not only the same man
but so happy in expressing them that each new
trait seemed to complete and enhance the others.

This third act contains the scene in which De
Mauprat, duped into the belief that Richelieu
in causing him to marry, has made him a mere
pander to the King, seeks the Cardinal's life
in revenge. When Macready, personating the
old and feeble man, encountered, without
recognizing him, the armed figure whose very
vizor was closed, and learned his deadly purpose,
nothing could be more intense and life-like,
nothing freer from inflation, than the glorious
arrogance with which he exclaimed—

> " Earth has no such fiend—
> No—as one parricide of his fatherland,
> Who dares in Richelieu murder France ! "

It should be noticed here that Macready carefully avoided the error into which some of his
successors have fallen—that of over-idealizing

Richelieu, by delivering his patriotic speeches
in such tones of exalted devotion as might have
befitted Brutus. Macready's apostrophes to
France, on the contrary, were given with a self-
reference, sometimes fierce in its expression, that
showed her triumphs to be part of his own. Her
glory was the object of his ambition, for it made
him great, while the thought that he laboured
for her consciously ennobled his ambition. Thus
his haughty boast in the foregoing lines was no
expression of abstract and ideal patriotism (of
which the Cardinal was incapable), but of
passionate and practical sympathy. How fine,
again, when De Mauprat, still unrecognized,
betrays that the dishonour put upon him has
made him an avenger, were the sudden gleam in
the eye, and the hushed tones of relief which
showed the statesman's sleepless vigilance at
that crisis—

"I breathe—he is no hireling!"

When, in this scene, De Mauprat reveals himself,
and Richelieu arrests his dagger by showing the
arts that have deluded him, the actor produced

one of those massive effects which make the
fortune of a drama. His commanding air, as he
motioned the dupe to his knees ; his rapid energy,
blent with a look of lofty pity, as he proclaimed
that, instead of planning dishonour for De
Mauprat's wife, he had saved her from it ; his
indignant look as, with tottering but imperial
step, he hurried to the door, and, summoning
Julie, confronted De Mauprat with the living
proof of his truth,—all this caused an excitement
which I have rarely seen equalled. It was
surpassed, however, by that supreme moment, in
the fourth act, when the might of Rome seemed
to pass into the sick man's frame, as he sprang up,
dominant and terrible, to shield Julie from the
King with the ægis of the Church. At this point
the vast pit seemed to rock with enthusiasm, as
it volleyed its admiration in rounds of thunder.
In the final scene of the fifth act, where the
Cardinal, apparently on the verge of death,
attends the King to resign, and to " render up the
ledgers of a realm," words can but faintly hint
the excellence of the performance. How touching

was the proud humility of the weak old man as
he relinquished, seemingly for ever, the splendid
cares of State; how arresting the sight of him
as, supported in his chair, his face now grew
vacant, as if through the feebleness of nature,
now resumed a gleam of intelligence, which at
times contracted into pain, as he gathered the
policy of his rivals—a policy fatal to France!
One noted the uneasy movements of the head,
the restless play of the wan fingers, though the
lips were silent, till at last the mind fairly
struggled awhile through its eclipse, as, in a loud
whisper, he warned the King his succours would
be wasted upon England.   Then came the
moment when, recovering the despatch which
convicted his foes of treason, he caused it to be
handed to the King, and sank supine with the
effort.   Slowly and intermittently consciousness
returned, as Louis thrice implored him to resume
his sway over France.   So naturally marked
were the fluctuations between life and death,
so subtly graduated (though comprised within
a few moments) were the signs of his recovery,

that the house utterly forgot its almost incredible quickness when, in answer to the King's apprehensive cry as to the traitors—

"Where will they be next week?"

Richelieu springs up resuscitated, and exclaims—

"There, at my feet!"

But it was not alone by acting, however fine, in this particular situation, that his triumph over probability was obtained. He had from the beginning of the play so seized every opportunity of identifying his fortunes and life with the greatness of his country, that when the King besought him to live for France, it seemed quite in the order of nature such an adjuration should have magical force. Who can forget the electrical rapidity and decision with which Macready, as the revivified minister, cut the Gordian knots of policy? The waiting envoys shall now have their answer. Chavigny, halting not for sleep or food, shall "arrest the Duc de Bouillon at the head of his armies." Baradas, who has "lost the stake," shall pay it and go out under guard. The barque of the State, but now tossing and plunging, a waif on the bosom of chance, has once more a helmsman, knows a course, and, through the sheer waters, bears on. And interests, dear though minor, confess the sudden change. Poor Julie, lately trembling for her husband's life, sees in his death writ but "parchment for battledores." The epicure and traitor, De Berrighen, scents danger to his dear health in the air of Paris. On François, the page who regained the despatch, again falls the smile that cheered and now rewards him. "He will never say fail again!" Ah, Joseph, trusty Joseph, bishop to be! The minister's policy—prompt action, daring, and retribution—the old man's fondness, the cynic's raillery, the patron's indulgence and humour,— this brilliant *résumé* of Richelieu throughout the play was so given, flash after flash, that its various effects seemed simultaneous rather than successive. Thus it was an audience dazzled, almost bewildered by the brilliancy of the achievement, that, on the instant fall of the curtain, burst into a roar of admiration that, wild, craving, unappeasable, pur-

sued, like a sea, the retreating actor, and swept
him back to the front.*

Pressing occupations and frequent absences from
town now for a time diverted my attention from
the theatres. When once more able to enjoy my
favourite recreation, I was, though but just of
age, a married man; I had published my first

---

* In his diary Macready speaks with some dissatisfaction of
his first night's performance of "Richelieu." But he was in the
habit, when anxious or dispirited, of underrating his work.
Thus when, after a lapse of time, he triumphantly resumed
his London representations of Iago (his early appearances in
the character had not been greatly successful), he was over-
whelmed with such a sense of failure, that his surprise next
morning to find his performance regarded as a masterpiece
must have been as great as his delight. The rapturous reception given to his first performance of "Richelieu," and the tone
of the press on the occasion, are vividly remembered by the
writer. It may be added that in the foregoing description
of "Richelieu," he has relied not only on his first youthful
impressions, but upon confirmatory ones drawn from many
later representations.

I may perhaps here be permitted to observe, for the benefit
of younger playgoers, that one of the best "Richelieus" since
Macready's, and the one that most recalls him, is that of Mr.
Edwin Booth. He gives the character a more modern air—
a greater air of *everyday* realism—than did Macready, though
realism of a certain kind was one of the latter's strongest
features. That Mr. Booth, however, is not deficient in the
more heroic aspects of the character, all who remember his
splendid acting at the end of the fourth act can abundantly
testify.

tragedy, and was anticipating an interview with
Macready, to whom it had been dedicated. Reports had reached me from his friends that he
contemplated the production of my play at Drury
Lane, of which he was recently become lessee,
while his letters to me, though they did not distinctly state such an intention, were pleasantly
consistent with it. To end suspense, I wrote to
him as to these reports, and immediately received
an answer, stating that they were well founded,
and inviting me to call upon him at the theatre.

These lines were written in October, 1885,
forty-four years after presenting myself for the
first time at Drury Lane Theatre. All the circumstances of my call are, however, as freshly present
to me as if it had been made yesterday—the
taciturn janitor who had probably been apprized
of my coming, and who, I fancied, regarded the
stripling visitor with civil astonishment; the boy
who was at once sent in with my card, and the
grave official who soon afterwards appeared from
the inner door of the theatre, and, saying in low
tones that Mr. Macready would be glad to see

the gentleman, requested me to follow him.   The vast stage—quite deserted at the time we crossed it—lay in a mid-day twilight, through which, nevertheless, one slanting ray of the outer sunshine clove sharply, striking with Rembrandt-like effect upon the dim and shrouded auditorium. More than once my guide warned me of scarcely visible obstructions, or indicated steps over which I should else have stumbled, speaking all the while in a tone of melancholy, mysterious dignity, as befitted one—for ever separated from the common herd—who, as connected with Drury Lane Theatre and its august manager, had prematurely gained the secret of life, and found that nothing was left to explore.   Doubtless my imagination had reflected on the worthy man its own romance; for to me this passage in life was nothing less than romance.   I was about to see not only Melantius, Virginius, and Richelieu, but Hamlet and Macbeth. It was like having an interview with Shakspere by proxy.   With such feelings I paused at the manager's room; the door opened, and I was in Macready's presence.   He sprang up from the

table at which he was writing, and gave me a
cordial welcome. Of the coldness and the assumption of dignity which I had heard ascribed to him
there was not a trace. Proud, no doubt, he was.
I had opportunities, later, of seeing him when some
unworthy taunt on his management or his acting
stung him more poignantly than might have been
expected, but his pride on these occasions took
the form of impetuous anger rather than of
haughtiness or contempt. But to proceed with
my impressions. His tall, imposing figure, his
expressive eye, his broad, massive brow (too
massive for beauty), might well have satisfied any
reasonable anticipation. If I felt a moment's disappointment, it must have been from some subtle
influence of association which made me seek to
identify him with his characters. I could hardly
have expected in private to see him in armour
or in a toga ; yet, absurd though the feeling was,
it seemed strange to me to find him in a frock
coat. I was immediately struck by the difference
between his voice in conversation and his clear
and musical articulation on the stage. He now

spoke in a kind of half-smothered bass, which, like his frequent pauses and self-corrections in talk, was too full of individuality to be unpleasing.

Our talk, of course, turned upon the play of mine which had been the means of introducing us. He was good enough to speak of it in very cordial terms, and to compliment me by remarking that my heroine would give some scope to the powers of Miss Helen Faucit, my warm admiration of whom he fully endorsed. After some discussion of the part intended for himself, he observed, "But, after all, your hero is young, and I doubt whether I should have the air of youth, especially in the dress of to-day.* Now, would you not prefer Mr. Anderson to play the character?" I should have been a very bad diplomatist had I assented to this suggestion; but, fortunately, I had no need of diplomacy, for my feelings ran in the same direction as my policy. I strongly expressed my disrelish of the proposal, adding that my chief pleasure in the production

* "The Patrician's Daughter," the play referred to, was one of then contemporary life.

of the piece would be gone if Mr. Macready himself did not appear as my hero. "The very thing to have said," observed an intimate friend of his when I related this little passage. "How much you would have dropped in his estimation had you taken him at his word!"

"Whether your piece will run," continued Macready, "is more than I can predict. It ends tragically; but audiences like a happy ending. Still, as I hope you know, this theatre is not conducted purely on principles of gain, but with some desire to encourage dramatic literature." On my assent to this, he resumed—"Of the fate of a play no amount of experience enables a man to judge. It is not always that even happy endings and capital construction insure success. Now, I may tell you," he said, in a confidential tone which inspired his young listener with all the complacent self-importance of one trusted with a State secret—"I may tell you that I played 'The Lady of Lyons' for a fortnight or three weeks to a serious loss, and that nothing but my sense of obligation to Bulwer, who had presented

the play to me in aid of the cause this theatre
supports, would have induced me to keep it in
the bills. Yet you see what a success it eventually became."

These remarks were probably intended to
moderate any over-sanguine views which I might
have formed respecting my own piece. The conversation then turned upon one or two of our
friends, and charmed with the tragedian in his
private character, and convinced that it must be
an unjust world in which such a man could find
detractors, I left the theatre.

CHAPTER III.

MACREADY—CONCLUSION.

Macready's friends and acquaintance—At dinner with him—
His guests—His first wife and his sister—Table-talk—
Browning's "Blot on the Scutcheon"—Opera of "Acis
and Galatea"—Its admirable cast—Unprecedented beauty
of its reproduction—Scenery by Stanfield—Invention of
a stage-sea with motion and sound—Compliment paid to
Macready by a lady on the production of the opera—
Pictures and picture-dealers—Pæstum and the Romans—
The poet Pope—Humorous reminiscences—Anecdote of
Porson—Macready a Liberal in politics—His objection to
the phrase, "lower classes"—An evening reception at his
house—Singing of Herr Staudigl in "Acis and Galatea"
—Assembly of celebrated authors, artists, etc.—Macready's
irritability at rehearsals, etc.—Author's impression that
this was to a great extent assumed—His King Lear—
This, in the writer's judgment, his greatest Shaksperian
performance—Detailed account of it—Macready's motto,
"Patience is genius," examined—Unjust to his own spontaneity—Walter Scott and Sheridan Knowles—Macready's
disparagement of Garrick—His theory that goodness was
essential to genius—His Macbeth—Regarded by his friends
as his *chef-d'œuvre*—Examination of his performance at
length—Also of his Hamlet—His Othello, Iago, Evelyn in
"Money"—His Benedick in "Much Ado"—His great
performance of Werner—Full account of it—Summary of
his various characters—His psychological insight and

artistic power of expressing emotion—His King John—His Shylock—Anecdote in note as to his revival of "King John" at Drury Lane—His Gisippus—His Spinola in "Nina Sforza"—His religious sentiment—The characters peculiarly suited to him—His defects and peculiarities—Comparison of him with contemporary actors—His intensity—In certain parts approaching Edmund Kean's—General estimate of his genius—His death.

THE guests at Macready's table were, in many cases, representative men and women, whose very presence was a testimony to the intellect and cultivation of their host. Besides being the friend, amongst writers, of Wordsworth, Thackeray, Dickens, Carlyle, Bulwer (the first Lord Lytton), Browning, Tennyson, John Forster, Mrs. Gore, Mrs. Norton, Lady Morgan ; amongst painters, of Stanfield, Maclise, Etty, and David Roberts, it may be said that few had obtained any marked reputation in literature or art without making his acquaintance. On the first day that my wife and myself dined with him, in 1842, we met, amongst others, Messrs. David Roberts, R.A., Boxall, Zouch, Troughton, author of " Nina Sforza ;" also, though his name is omitted in Macready's diary for the day, John Elliotson, M.D., an able physician who

dared to think for himself, and whose treatment
was often as brilliantly successful as original,
though his advocacy of mesmerism roused much
opposition and controversy, and was looked upon
at the time as heterodox by his professional
brethren.

Here a word of pleasant recollection may be
given to the wife and sister of the tragedian.
The first Mrs. Macready, the " Kitty Atkins " of
his father's company, possessed that union of
gentleness with cordiality which is always most
winning.   There was a sweetness in her counte-
nance and a delicate grace in her manner
peculiarly feminine.   I had the pleasure of taking
in Miss Macready, who showed no little observation and genial humour.   She had much of her
brother's quick perception, with a playfulness
of expression very rare with him, though very
charming when displayed.

The conversation turned very little upon the
drama or the theatre, though, in the course of
the evening, Macready adverted with emphatic
admiration to an unpublished play by Robert

Browning. It was, I believe, "The Blot on the
Scutcheon," subsequently performed at Drury
Lane—a work which, in point of passion and that
noble utterance in which reality and imagination
blend, yields to none in the series of great plays
with which the most profound and poetical
dramatist since Shakspere has enriched our
literature. A passing reference was also made
to the late reproduction of "Acis and Galatea"
at Drury Lane. The presentation of this opera
was one of the great triumphs of Macready's
management, first, on account of its splendid
cast, which included the famous Herr Staudigl,
Allen, Miss P. Horton, and Miss Romer. As
a frame for this opera, too, Stanfield had out-
done himself in the exquisite scenery which he
painted, in token of his admiration and friendship
for the lessee of Drury Lane. Amongst other
remarkable features was the invention of a stage-
sea, which admirably imitated a natural one, both
in sound and motion, and which, when the curtain
rose on its solitude at the opening, was ecstatically
applauded by the audience, as though it had been

a distinguished actor. Macready remarked that he had never been more delighted than by a compliment paid him by a lady in reference to this production. " Now," said she, " I have *seen* a poem." The talk turned, however, for the most part upon subjects interesting to the scholar or the virtuoso—upon the various signs by which copies of the old masters, pretending to be originals, might be detected, upon ancient Pæstum and its attractions as a Roman resort, upon Pope, the poet, and his merits. These somewhat grave topics found occasional and still dignified relief in anecdotes of picture-buyers, who had either been imposed upon by fraudulent vendors, or who had baffled them more than once, in a humorous reminiscence of travel, and in an anecdote of Porson, the particulars of which I caught indistinctly; but I believe they referred to the singularity of a man of his pursuits and tastes having written a farce.

During dinner a lady happened to speak of the " lower classes "—a phrase to which Macready excepted. " Will you let me," he said, " correct that expression? I always like to think of our less fortunate fellow-creatures as the *poorer* classes, rather than as the *lower* classes." Perhaps a conventional phrase uttered by a lady at dinner hardly needed so grave a comment, but there is no doubt that Macready was thoroughly sincere in making it. Those who knew him more intimately than I did have often testified to his earnest sympathy with the people—a sympathy which seems at first sight a little inconsistent with his overbearing manner, at times, to his subordinates in the theatre. About two months later we had the pleasure of hearing Herr Staudigl in several of the *morceaux* of Polyphemus, in "Acis and Galatea." A company of celebrities was present, amongst others, Carlyle, Browning, Procter (Barry Cornwall), John Forster, Sir M. A. Shee, President of the Royal Academy, Sir Edwin Landseer, R.A., Sir Charles and Lady Morgan, Lady Stepney, etc.

I chanced to be present at Drury Lane on an occasion when Macready was conducting a rehearsal of " King John." The groupings of that

play, and the stage business in general, were
elaborate enough to account for, and almost excuse
the manager's impatience. Very striking, however,
was his sudden change from angry excitement,
when addressing his "supers," to his unruffled
courtesy of tone and look when he turned to
myself or others of his acquaintance on the stage.
It was, of course, not the fact of the change, but
its instantaneousness, that was remarkable. From
that day I conceived an impression, which still
remains, that his bursts of temper were far more
under his control than perhaps he himself supposed, and that he was sometimes inclined to
exaggerate them that they might contrast with
his after-smoothness—that he was exhibiting, in
short, his beloved stage transitions in real life.
I do not in the least mean to deny his excitable
temper, which a Drury Lane rehearsal was of all
things likely to call forth; but to suggest that
its manifestations were less serious than they
appeared, and that he perhaps showed off its
starts and sallies to excess, that his skill in
reining it in might be the more obvious.

It is now time to revert to his performances.
His King Lear, as I saw it in his later days,
when it had acquired a broader and more
masculine outline than before, was, I think,
his finest achievement in Shaksperian tragedy.
With that poetic power of symbolism which
was one of his especial gifts, there was, on his
first entrance, in his accents, sovereignly imperious, and in his free, large movements (though
the gait at times gave just a hint of age), the
outward and visible sign, not only of Lear's
strong and absolute will, but of the primitive,
half-savage royalty that we associate with remote
and legendary periods. He was still a hale and
zealous hunter, not unwilling, indeed, to forego
the toils of State, but bribed to do so, before
the full need came, by prodigal love for his
children. If he became, afterwards, " a very feeble,
fond old man," it was ingratitude, not the weight
of years, that had thus undone him. There were
many fine touches of nature in the first act.
One of these was especially subtle. Lear has
repudiated his once idolized Cordelia; he would

fain forget her, and speak of his future plans.
But, in striving to do this, his voice suddenly
for a moment broke, then to the end of
the sentence hardened into inflexibility. Very
striking, too, was the King's demeanour just
afterwards, when Kent remonstrates. His anger
first showed itself in an ominous tone of warning
which arrested and awed—

"The bow is bent and drawn; make from the shaft;"

then, as the faithful adherent persisted, it swelled
into a mingling of amazement, scorn, and con-
vulsive rage, that would have befitted a Cæsar,
flattered into the belief of his divinity, and swift
to punish opposition as impious. The curse
which ends the act struck terror by its still
intensity, and the change from wrath to agony
at the words—

"That she may feel
How sharper than a serpent's tooth it is
To have a thankless child,"

almost excused the malediction. To specify all
the striking details of this great performance
would need an entire essay. It may be said,

in brief, that as the boundless arrogance of Lear
was the sin by which he fell, so a revelation to
the old man's heart—even through his disordered
wits—of the common ties of our humanity was,
with Macready, the great lesson of the play.
Thus he threw into even unusual relief those
noble passages in which the poet contrasts the
lots of rich and poor, of oppressor and thrall,
or in which he shows the nothingness of mortal
man at his best, when he encounters the forces
of Nature or Circumstance.   In the storm-scene,
where Lear's madness is yet incipient, and in
the still more terrible disclosure of the fourth
act, Macready was on ground (that of psychology),
where, if we except a few inspired characters of
Edmund Kean, he seemed unapproachable.   His
dawning insanity gleamed out in his almost
parental tenderness to the fool, as if he felt
instinctively the bond between them.   The
recurrence to a fixed idea, in his obstinate and,
at last, passionate asseveration that Edgar's
" unkind daughters " were the cause of his
affliction, might, for its air of penetration and

good faith, have been set down in the diagnosis
of a physician. When complete aberration set
in, the signs of it were astonishingly true and
various. The keen, over-eager attention, the
sudden diversion to new excitements, the light
garrulousness, the unmeaning smile, or the
abstracted silence, denoted by turns so many
shifting moods of fantasy through which one
torturing recollection, like a knell, heard in brief
lulls of winds and waters, broke ever and anon.
His gradual recognition of Cordelia, as the mists
of delusion gradually lifted and dissolved, was
a worthy climax to such a performance. Her
well-known voice, her tender words, at first fixed
him as with a sweet but vague and bewildering
consciousness :—

> " You do me wrong to take me out of the grave.
> Thou art a soul in bliss, but I am bound
> Upon a wheel of fire.
>
>   .   .   .   .   .
>
> You are a spirit, I know ; when did you die ? "

Then, how fine was the struggle towards memory
and definite perception! What effort, what
despondency in the failure!

"I should e'en die with pity
To see another thus."

And, finally, how true, how overpowering, the
expression of yearning hope which he almost
feared to test, as he sank trembling into her
embrace!—

"Do not laugh at me,
For, as I am a man, I think this lady
To be my child, Cordelia."

It is in such a delineation as this that the
actor (precluded from any great originality in
the *conception* of the character laid down for
him) becomes in his turn almost creative, by
translating the poet's ideas into an appropriate
language of looks, tones, and gestures, which
make that living and incarnate which was comparatively but abstract and intellectual.   For
such a rendering, patient observation is no less
needed than sympathetic impulse.   I have more
than once heard Macready say, "Patience is
genius"—a sentiment which, I think, originally
belongs to Montaigne.   Yet patience, though a
proof of the interest and fortitude which genius
begets, can hardly be genius itself.   The tra-

gedian, I sometimes thought, did some injustice
to his own spontaneity in insisting almost
exclusively upon the value of hard work. The
truth is, he found in mental activity not only
a duty but a delight. His love of painting,
his wide acquaintance with literature, the charm
which psychology had for him, as evinced not
only in his acting, where motive and character
were so finely laid bare, but in the fascination
of Browning's poetry, showed a warmth and
extent of sympathy without which patience
would have lacked its best incentive and yielded
but frigid results. He was more of an enthusiast
than he himself believed. One night the discussion turned upon Sir Walter Scott, and his
inability as a dramatist, and why, with all his
powers of characterization and situation in narrative, he had never written a play likely to move
an audience. " I suppose he did not choose," said
one of the party. " Choose ! " broke in Macready,
warmly ; " it's no matter of choice. If he had
had the true dramatic fire, he couldn't have
suppressed it. So says Knowles, and I echo

him," thus showing that in his deepest convictions, his favourite patience, though sometimes a sign of genius, was no substitute for it.

On the night in question, the after-dinner talk turned upon celebrated past actors, especially upon Garrick, of whom I thought Macready spoke with undue severity. In doing so, he broached a theory which will, I fancy, be generally disputed. " I will not believe," said he, " that a man so avaricious and self-seeking * could have been a great actor." It was contended, on the other side, that there were abundant instances in which the moral defects of men had not prevented their greatness as artists. " Meanness and selfishness," he rejoined, " must affect their *sincerity*. They cannot express with full power by mere intellect the nobler emotions with which they have no real sympathy." Here I asked whether, if this doctrine were true, it would not lead also to the conclusion that a good man must fail in the portraiture of evil, and

* Surely this is a harsher verdict upon Garrick than is warranted by the facts known of him, viewed as a whole.

that the actor must be morally bad who could
paint bad characters—Iago, for instance, or
Richard the Third. "No; that will not hold,"
he said. "Whoever has fine qualities can paint
the base;" meaning, I suppose, that he could
paint them as opposites. It was, at all events,
pleasant to find Macready attaching so much
value to moral character in relation to art.
Though it is difficult to accept his view in its
full extent, there may be a measure of truth
in it. A selfish man may be very sincere in
declaiming a fine burst of feeling, or even in
portraying a fine nature generally; yet it is at
least possible that habitual loyalty to right may
give a force of conviction to the expression of
it quite beyond the reach of merely sentimental
approval.

The leading tragedies of Shakspere were then
discussed. "Macbeth," in addition to its grandeur
of imagination, was voted his most perfect
play for the stage. Various allusions to our
host's embodiment of the guilty Thane led
to the inference that it was regarded as his

chef-d'œuvre. I could not altogether subscribe
to that opinion, my reasons for which will appear
in the account I shall now give of his performance.

Of all Macready's representations, that of
Macbeth probably most satisfied himself. He
had performed no Shaksperian character more
frequently; it was that, moreover, in which he
took his leave of the stage. Though it never
realized my ideal, I learned, as I grew in years,
to appreciate its many excellences. After the
departure of the witches, in the first act, the air
of brooding reverie in the soliloquy, with a
strange sense conveyed in the fixed and fateful
gaze of impending evil, the insidious encroach-
ment of evil, spite of brief but terrible recoil,
and afterwards the overdone warmth with which
he excuses his abstraction to Rosse and Angus,
were rendered with consummate skill and effect.
In the scenes where Lady Macbeth prompts him
to the murder, his resistance seemed somewhat
too feeble for the remorse he has afterwards to
display. " One of John Kemble's most effective

passages," said that fine critic, W. J. Fox, "was the one beginning—

"'We will proceed no further in this business,'
which he uttered with such a sigh of relief and thankfulness, it seemed to bear away with it a crushing load and to leave him renewed and hopeful." The apostrophe to the "air-drawn dagger," as given by Macready, was a triumph of discrimination and emphasis. The transitions from amazement and awe to reviving reason— once more staggered by the growing force of his terrors, and again reasserting itself to dispel them —could not have been more judiciously marked. And yet—to me, at least—there seemed a want. Reasoning carried it over intuition; all had been too obviously reasoned out. The thoughts did not sufficiently hurry upon and partly confuse each other, as they do in real tumults of the soul. The crouching form and stealthy, felon-like step of the self-abased murderer, as he quitted the scene, made, however, a picture not to be forgotten. In contrast with the erect, martial figure that entered in the first act, this change was the

moral of the play made visible. The acting of
Macready, after the murder, has been so generally
extolled, that I rather state as a personal feeling
than as a critical opinion that here again various
mental states seemed too sharply defined and separated. The emotions of shame, terror, remorse,
momentary despair, and selfish fear, might, I
fancied, have more often flowed into each other,
as when, in real life, some fatal act almost at the
same moment excites and yet paralyzes apprehension by the sense that it is irretrievable. I
thought of Hazlitt's description of Edmund Kean
at this point. "The hesitation, the bewildered
look, the coming to himself when he sees his
hands bloody; the manner in which his voice
clung to his throat and choked his utterance;
his agony and tears, the force of nature overcome
by passion — beggared description." Something
of this I missed in Macready, though his entire
performance was probably finer and more suggestive than that of Kean. But Macready's final
waking to the full conviction of the gulf between
the past and the present was one of his grandest

moments.   I still vividly recall the terrible agony
of his cry—

" Wake Duncan with thy knocking ; I would thou couldst ! "

as, with his face averted from his wife, and his
arms outstretched, as it were, to the irrecoverable
past, she dragged him from the stage.

The entrance of Banquo's ghost in the third
act gives an opportunity to a tragic actor of
which Macready fully availed himself.   His
great merit, however, in this act, was the force
with which he previously brought out the gnaw-
ings of conscience and the insecurity of ill-gotten
power.   In his haggard aspect, in his restless
movements, it seemed as if the curse, " Macbeth
shall sleep no more," had taken visible effect.
What misery pierced through his hollow mirth
when he exclaimed—

" But let the frame of things disjoint, both the worlds suffer,
   Ere we will eat our meal in fear,"

feigning so quickly followed by his tones of
hopeless yearning in the words—

" Duncan is in his grave,
After life's fitful fever *he* sleeps well."

When his wife questioned him as to Banquo, the furtive look with which he turned from the very partner of his crime bore terrible witness to the isolation of guilt. The sinister, ill-suppressed laugh which accompanied his answer—

> " Be innocent of knowledge, dearest chuck,
> Till thou applaud the deed ! "

marked, I thought, a new and dreadful stage in the usurper's experience. What a revelation in the words, *" dearest chuck "* ! She whose spirit had so dominated his in the early scenes was now his mere half-trusted accomplice. His misery had cast off awe ; he was become grimly familiar with her. His much applauded transition in the last act, from the impetuous command to Seyton, " Give me mine armour," to the ultra-colloquial, " How does your patient, doctor ? " never appeared to me a beauty. It was a telling stage-contrast, but so extreme as to be factitious. His closing scenes could not have been surpassed. His physical energy was terrific, and took grandeur from the desperate mind. He turned upon Fate and stood at bay.

Comparing his Macbeth with his Hamlet, I retain to the last a preference for the latter, though even at the time I first saw it he scarcely looked the character. His tall figure, with its large and bold outlines, his brow, almost ample enough to be ponderous, hardly suggested the refined, pensive prince who was yet "the glass of fashion and the mould of form." And, indeed, Hamlet, as interpreted by this tragedian, was less the melancholy, musing Dane than he is generally represented. There was more of passion than of sentiment in the rendering. With Macready, the credulous faith, so bitterly dispelled, of the young optimist, was turned to gall. Thus, to the end of the third act, a tone of glowing excitement or of keen irony were the features of the embodiment. Except for a touch of melancholy tenderness for a lost ideal in Ophelia, or of the courtesy which his princely nature prescribed to his inferiors, Hamlet was, with him, a misanthrope. It was only when he had long writhed under the sense of human wrong and "the yoke of-inauspicious stars" that his mind, driven back upon its early instinct of faith, grew patient and trustful, in spite of experience. " We defy augury. There is a special providence in the fall of a sparrow. . . . The readiness is all." Conversing with a friend, he once observed, " In the early acts of ' Hamlet' I seek to express, among other things, the impetuous rebellion of a generous nature when its trust has been cruelly deceived; in the last act, the resignation of a generous nature when the storm has spent itself;—in presenting the striking contrasts of this conception—its passion, its imagination, its irony, its colloquial realism." On the appearance of the Ghost, his voice and manner so expressed a soul spellbound and set apart from men by a supernatural visitation as to hold the house breathless with awe. In the celebrated scene with Ophelia, true to his theory of the optimist turned pessimist, he was far more bitter than Charles Kemble or Charles Kean, yet the agony of his love pierced through the bitterness. In the closet-scene, though gentle at the close, he was sterner to his mother than were his stage contemporaries. His indictment of her was

delivered with an arresting concentration that
had nothing in it of violence or tumult, and with
a mien lofty and unrelenting, as if he had been
the commissioned angel of retribution.   His
acting in the play scene was superb.   His answers
to the King's suspicious questions, as the play
before the Court proceeds, were keen, glittering,
and venomous, like the thrusts of a poisoned
dagger.   With body prone, and head erect, and
eyes riveted on Claudius, he dragged himself
nearer and nearer to him, till the moment of Gon-
zago's murder, then sprang up to meet the convicted King, with a burst of mocking exultation.
His performance abounded, moreover, with delicate
and poetic suggestions.   One of these was his way
of quitting the stage at the end of the first act,
after his interview with the Ghost.   About to
depart, he turned to Horatio and Marcellus, and
saying, in a tone tender and hushed, " Nay, come,
let's go together," led them off the stage.   Being
at the same hotel with him in Manchester, I went
into his room one night after returning from his
performance of Hamlet.   I remarked that this act

of fellowship on the part of Hamlet had greatly struck me, as indicating the sense of brother-hood between man and man which the awe of a supernatural visitation would call forth. This comment pleased him. " It is one of those minute touches," he replied, "that an actor throws in only after long familiarity with a part. As to Hamlet, I believe no man ever played it with any approach to completeness until he was too old to look it."

His Othello, though some of the details were masterly, could not, I think, be considered a great success. His indignant passion was at times most powerful, but it was a passion into which the agony of deceived love too little entered. It was rather the cry of betrayed honour than of a tortured heart. Among his fine points was the thrusting of his dark, despairing face through the curtains of the bed when Emilia calls to him after Desdemona's murder. The discovery of the face alone — "the index to a tragic volume "—was thrilling in its effect, besides forming incidentally, in contrast with the drapery, a marvellous piece of colour. Macready may have had no misgivings as to the claims of his Othello, but I think he understood its comparative unpopularity. One morning, after the tragedy had been some days announced, he said to me in the theatre, with his smile of austere humour, "I am about to punish an undiscerning public. They will not see my Othello next week." A poor "let" had doubtless induced him to postpone it.

His Iago, on the other hand, was one of his most famous delineations. With absorbing self-love and the vindictiveness it engenders for its chief motives, was combined delight in evil activity of intellect. It was the knave's pastime with Macready to become, in appearance, "all things to all men"—bluntly faithful and disinterested with Othello, genial comrade with Cassio, loose gallant with Roderigo, amusing cynic with Desdemona. In some of these phases, though assumed only to further a dark purpose, an admirable vein of comedy was evinced.

His incidental touches of comedy in serious

characters were, indeed, very characteristic and
happy. Amongst these may be ranked, besides
the hypocritical phases of Iago, his playful raillery
of the love-struck Virginia, his downright soldierly
frankness in Melantius, his easy gaiety with the
players, his courtly but incisive irony towards the
spies in Hamlet. In all characters that combined
the keen perception of human meanness and
inconsistency with social courtesy in expressing
it, he was thoroughly at home. Thus his representation of Evelyn, with his clever cynicism,
in Lord Lytton's "Money," was an incontestable
success. He somewhat underrated, I think, the
great opportunities which the part afforded him.
" I should never have performed Evelyn," he said,
" had it not been written by Bulwer."

In one celebrated character in Shaksperian
comedy he gained a triumph which, in its way,
might fairly rank with any that he achieved in
tragedy. The character was that of Benedick,
which he played for his benefit. In this part his
spontaneous humour, especially in the scene
where he resolves to marry, roused the house to

such shouts of mirth, one might have thought
Keeley, not Macready, was on the stage.   His
Benedick differed widely from that of other
well-known actors.   Whether it was the truest
rendering of the part may be doubted, but I
have seen none more effective.   In the various
conflicts with Beatrice there was not that eagerness of repartee, that animated enjoyment of the
wit combat, nor quite that polished address
(though Macready was both the soldier and the
gentleman) ascribed to Charles Kemble.   Macready had rather a provokingly indulgent and
half-careless air towards his fair enemy.   He
wore a somewhat *blasé* manner to her, as of one
versed in the serious business of life, and a little
cynical through experience, who, nevertheless,
good-naturedly consented to trifle and *badiner*
with a lady for her amusement, who sometimes
forgets his light *rôle* in serious thought, and then,
rousing himself, returns apologetically to his recreation.   In the celebrated soliloquy in the second
act, after he has overheard in the arbour that
Beatrice loves him, the complex expression of

his face as he advanced drew roars from the
house before he uttered a word.   One might read
there the sense of amazement, of gratification,
and of perplexity as to the way of reconciling
his newly-revealed passion for Beatrice with his
late raillery at her and all women.   His amazement was less, even, that Beatrice loved him, than
that (his suspicion deepening to conviction as
the soliloquy went on) he responded to her love.
He evidently remembered his own recent vaunt,
" I do much wonder that one man, seeing how
much another is a fool when he dedicates his
behaviours to love, will, after he hath laughed at
such shallow follies in others, become the argument of his own scorn by falling in love."
Accordingly, Macready, with great humour, made
Benedick, in his first wish to be consistent, put
his response to Beatrice rather upon the ground
of pity and courtesy than of his own strong
inclining : " Love me ! why it must be requited.
I hear how I am censured "—a shallow sophism to
disguise his passion, which again called forth the
heartiest mirth.   His next step in reasoning,

where he makes a moral aphorism the pretext for yielding to his inclinations, " Happy are they that hear their detractions, and can put them to mending," was not a whit less effective. In fact, the humour of the position, from his first surprise and timid regard for his consistency to the defiant scorn of ridicule at the close, was splendidly brought out. The most specious argument acquired with him the force of reason, or, if not, his will dispensed with it. It was an unopposed march, in which the victor gains audacity as he takes outwork upon outwork, until he hoists his flag from the citadel.

The success of the tragedian in this brilliant comedy was complete; yet he had so much doubted of it beforehand, he said, that he had proposed resigning Benedick to Mr. Anderson after the first night. He had had, as we have seen, similar misgivings with respect to Iago, and, previously to resuming the part in London, had been wretched with the apprehension of failure. The acclamations of the audience and the verdict of the best critics on Benedick, which proved to be one of his finest impersonations, came upon him as a shock of pleasure.

Among Macready's triumphs his Werner holds so high a place as to require some minuteness of detail. Of all his characters out of Shakspere (and I do not forget Virginius or Melantius), Werner and Richelieu are those which most often recur to me. Amiable censors have not been wanting to allege that his success in Werner was chiefly due to the resemblance between the hero of the drama and himself in point of morbid pride and sensitiveness. This theory, however, by no means accounts for the impressive melancholy which he wore when Werner's honours were restored, or, above all, for that display of a father's love and agony in the fifth act, which must be ranked amongst his supreme effects. But to whatever cause his exhibition of pride and bitter, querulous impatience, in the first act, were due, it is hard to conceive of their being more intense and incisive. The rising of the curtain discovered the fugitive nobleman, indignant at his cruel fate, stalking to and fro like

some captured wild animal in his cage. The
gaunt look of recent sickness was in his face, the
fretful irritability which it causes repeatedly
broke forth, spite of his affection for his wife, in
his tones and gestures; while, through the veil
of poverty, disease, and mental suffering, gleamed
a forlorn haughtiness of bearing which bespoke
his ineradicable pride of birth. The quick apprehensions and suspicions which spring from nerves
wasted alike with disease and grief were admirably conveyed, first, by his alarm when he hears
the knocking of the Intendant, and again, by the
air of feline wariness and distrust with which he
scanned Gabor on his entrance and subsequently.
At length Stralenheim enters, who seeks to usurp
Werner's domain, and, for that evil end, to secure
his person. Werner at once recognizes him, and
the former has at length a dim suspicion that the
man before him is his intended victim. When
at length Stralenheim turns to him, after conversing with the Intendant and Gabor, the furtive
and apprehensive gaze with which Macready had
watched his oppressor, gave way to irrepressible

hatred. Nothing could be more curtly repellant than his tones, in answer to Stralenheim's questions—

> "*Stral.* Have you been here long?
> *Wer.* (*with abrupt surprise*).   Long?
> *Stral.*   I sought
> An answer, not an echo.
> *Wer.* (*rapidly and morosely*). You may seek
> Both from the walls; I am not used to answer
> Those whom I know not."

A little later, when Stralenheim observes, " Your language is above your station," Werner's answer, " *Is it?* " contained a transition from ironical humility to scorn and loathing, which it was surprising so brief a phrase could express. Not less striking, when he feared his passion might betray him, was the sudden change, in the words that follow, to rude and caustic indifference—

> " 'Tis well that it is not beneath it,
> As sometimes happens to the better clad."

In the second act, it will be remembered that Werner, made desperate by the plain suspicions of Stralenheim, who has power to arrest and imprison him, commits a robbery on his foe, in

the dead of night, to gain the means of escape.
Subsequently, Werner and his wife are discovered
by their long-lost son, Ulric.   The joy of the
parents has scarcely found utterance when Ulric
tells them that he had, on the previous day,
saved the life of Stralenheim, and that he is now
in quest of the villain who had robbed him.   To
give any conception of Macready's acting at this
point, I must quote the dialogue—

" *Wer.* (*agitatedly*).   Who
Taught you to mouth that name of ' villain ? '
     Ulr.   What
More noble name belongs to common thieves ?
     Wer. Who taught you thus to brand an unknown being
With an infernal stigma ?
     Ulr.   My own feelings
Taught me to name a ruffian from his deeds.
     Wer. Who taught you, long-sought and ill-found boy ! that
It would be safe for my own son to insult me ?
     Ulr. I named a villain.   What is there in common
With such a being and my father ?
     Wer.   Everything !
That ruffian *is* thy father.
     Jos.   Oh, my son !
Believe him not—and yet !—— (*her voice falters*).
     Ulr. (*starts, looks earnestly at* WERNER, *and then says slowly*).
                              And you avow it ?
     Wer. Ulric ! Before you dare despise your father,
Learn to divine and judge his actions. Young,
Rash, new to life, and reared in luxury's lap,
Is it for you to measure passion's force,

Or misery's temptation? Wait—(not long,
It cometh like the night, and quickly)—Wait!—
Wait till, like me, your hopes are blighted—till
Sorrow and shame are handmaids of your cabin;
Famine and poverty your guests at table;
Despair your bed-fellow—then rise, but not
From sleep, and judge! Should that day e'er arrive—
Should you see then the serpent who hath coiled
Himself around all that is dear and noble
Of you and yours, lie slumbering in your path,
With but *his* folds between your steps and happiness,
When *he*, who lives but to tear from you name,
Lands, life itself, lies at your mercy, with
Chance your conductor; midnight for your mantle;
The bare knife in your hand, and earth asleep,
Even to your deadliest foe; and he, as 'twere,
Inviting death, by looking like it, while
His death alone can save you :—Thank your God!
If then, like me, content with petty plunder,
You turn aside—*I* did so!"

From the cry of remonstrance with which the
above passage opens, even to its close, what a
complexity of emotions struggling and, at the
same time, blending with each other, did Macready portray! The strife between wrathful
pride and agony, at having to confess and
extenuate his guilt to his idolized and just-
regained son; the increasing and, at last, breathless rapidity with which he piled up the circumstances of his desperate temptation and venial

sin; till, finallv, pride, self-abasement, and self-
vindication were swallowed up and swept away
by a master-touch of paternal love and anguish,
as, shaken, convulsed, with extended arms and
bowed head, he appealed to Ulric with the words,
"*I* did so;"—all these, with their harrowing
pathos and subduing power, live in my memory
as if they were of yesterday. More than forty
years have not weakened their effect.

The bald tale, in the third act, of Stralenheim's
murder by an unknown hand, of Werner's dread
lest he should be suspected of the crime, and of
his escape from the spot, supply little that is of
dramatic interest.   The fourth act, also, which
shows Werner restored to his estates and to his
title of Count Siegendorf, moves slowly and
eventlessly, though the sense of heartsick grief
for unrequited affection could not have found
more faithful expression than in the scene where
the restored Count bewails the coldness of the
son in whom his every hope was centred.   His
grief here had low and level tones, as if it had
gradually sapped and well-nigh exhausted the

active force of emotion. There was a forlornness, a vain, wasting craving in his look, a restlessness which his brave robes as Count seemed to intensify by contrast. The fifth act, however, brings the great situation of the tragedy. In his disguise as Werner, before flying, after Stralenheim's death, Count Siegendorf had, it will be remembered, met Gabor, a Hungarian. He has deeply suspected this man of being Stralenheim's murderer. At the celebration of a national festival in Prague, he has seen him in the crowd. Soon afterwards the supposed criminal, instead of avoiding detection, repairs to the Count's mansion and demands to see him. He is admitted, and answers Siegendorf's charge of murder by accusing Ulric of it, who is present. The Count, drawing, rushes on Gabor with fierce indignation, then turns from him with incredulous disdain. The latter, however, proceeds with his story. What Macready achieved here in the way of facial expression and symbolic gesture (for his share in the dialogue was small), has never, I think, under the given condition, been exceeded.

At first, with one arm thrown fondly round his son's shoulder, he listened with light scorn to his accuser. As the proofs thickened, the eyes, before careless, became fixed on Gabor. This man related particular after particular, the fearful significance of which against his son the Count at length recognized, while the relaxed arm which lay on Ulric's shoulder fell heavily. As Gabor proceeded, and with increasing stress of proof, the Count turned and looked at his son. Shocked by his expression, he faltered a step from him. The tale continued, and again the stricken father unconsciously fell back. His changes of look and attitude had silently told all the effects of the story upon the sympathizing spectators.

As I have said, the words allotted here to Macready were few and far between; but there was little need of words. The changes in the father's heart were uttered in a tongue of which every movement was a syllable, every look an accent.

At length Gabor retires, and Count Siegendorf is left alone with Ulric, who not only confesses the murder, but urges the "silencing of Gabor."

While the father lies horror-struck in his chair,
Ulric proceeds to explain and defend his crime
in slaying Stralenheim. When the Count answers
him with expressions of grief and abhorrence,
Ulric retorts thus—

> "If *you* condemn me, yet
> Remember *who* hath taught me, once too often,
> To listen to him! *Who* proclaimed to me
> That *there were crimes made venial by the occasion?*"

The greatness of Macready's acting here reached
its climax. As Ulric cited the fatal doctrine of
expediency, by which Siegendorf had extenuated
his robbery in the second act, the feeling that his
own maxims and example had betrayed his son
into crime was fearfully expressed by the con-
vulsions of the face, by the hands, that first
sought to close the ears, and then to beat back
the fatal sounds that would enter. When at
length Ulric, in plain terms, charges his disgrace
upon his father's precepts, Macready produced
one of those rare effects which become traditions
of the theatre. With a shrill cry of agony, as if
pierced mortally by a dart, he bounded from his
seat, and then, as if all strength had failed him,

wavered and fluttered forward, so to speak, till he sank on one knee in front of the stage.*

How various are the characters, some of them especially identified with him, which the name of this great artist recalls;—in Shakspere, Lear, Hamlet, Macbeth, King John, Henry the Fourth, Iago, Iachimo, Prospero, Benedick, the Fifth Harry, with his impetuous chivalry, Brutus, with his placid self-devotion, his long forbearance with Cassius, his noble and tender fortitude in Portia's loss, and his indulgent care for his drowsy attendant; in the general drama, Melantius, in "The Bridal," the soul of honour, Virginius, the father-priest, Richelieu, wily, imperious, patriotic, Ion, the antique type of youth

---

* Mr. Macready was succeeded in his great performance of Werner by Mr. Phelps, who played the character with considerable effect during his management of Sadler's Wells. Since then, Werner remained unrepresented by any adequate actor, until it was revived by Mr. Henry Irving, on June 1, 1887, for the benefit of the present writer, with a sympathetic generosity that has scarcely a parallel in theatrical annals. The pathetic watchfulness of the father absorbed in his son, and the overpowering climax of paternal agony when Ulric's unworthiness is at length discovered, have been recorded with due appreciation and delight by other pens than that of the writer.

in its beauty and self-sacrifice, Claude Melnotte,
the modern type of youth in its bright credulity
and passionate impulse. If, as has been said, he
was in this last character here and there a little
too weighty and tragic, the wonder yet was that
at his years, and with his serious bias, his performance was on the whole so elastic, flexible, and
spirited.

Of the qualities to which Macready owed his
eminence, the highest and most remarkable were
his psychological insight and his artistic power
of translating his emotions into strikingly
appropriate—often absolutely symbolic—forms
of expression. If it be granted that one or two
tragedians have, in some parts, excelled him in the
sudden revelations of passion, it is yet probable
that he has never been excelled, if equalled,
in the complete and harmonious development
of character. In all his great impersonations
was shown the same faculty of grasping the
central idea of his part, and of making all the
lights thrown upon details correspond with that
idea. What has already been said of his Lear,

Hamlet, and Macbeth, will suggest how finely
the faculty just referred to was evinced in these
impersonations. His King John furnishes another
marked example. Before practising for Arthur's
death, the Usurper was still a Plantagenet,
haughty and martial in bearing, swift and bold
in decision. After the abasement of instigating
murder, the whole bearing of the man changed;
the former knight had caught something of the
dogged, covert look, the bowed form, the stealthy
gait of the assassin. When, in the fifth act,
Faulconbridge attempts to rekindle the spirit of
the soldier in John, his answer, in feeble,
disheartened tones, "Have *thou* the ordering of
this present time," was "a whole history."
Dignity and will had forsaken him. Except in
remorse, he was a Plantagenet no more.*

---

* In the revival of "King John," in 1841, Macready introduced a new effect. After the fight in the third act, which
results in an English victory, a part of the English force
crossed the stage, preceded by trumpeters, who sounded notes
of melancholy and wailing. One night, at Macready's house,
Mr. W. J. Fox objected that sounds of this kind could not with
propriety have proceeded from the triumphant English, the
retreat alluded to in the stage directions being clearly that of
the French. Macready answered that the purpose of these

An instance of his subtle blending of the chief
motives of a part with its national features, was
to be found in his Shylock, where the Jew's
traditional reverence for law, and belief in its
inviolability, were emphasized in his delineation:
" I stand for judgment; answer, shall I have it ? "
" If you deny me, fie upon your law." " I crave
the law." " I charge you by the law." " You
know the law; your exposition hath been most
sound." " Is that the law ? "

The power of expressing states of feeling by
gesture and attitude is, of course, necessary to
every actor. With Macready it rose into a
special endowment. Take two more examples
of this, the first from Gerald Griffin's almost
forgotten play of " Gisippus," produced at Drury
Lane. On discovering that his betrothed, whom
he passionately loves, is really attached to his

notes was to prepare the house for King John's sinister interview with Hubert, which immediately followed. On being
asked for my opinion—that of a very young man—by two who
were greatly my seniors, I was diplomatic enough to observe
that the question seemed to be how far a dramatic effect,
finely suggestive, might be purchased at the expense of
probability.

friend, Gisippus, after a struggle, resigns her to him. The marriage day comes, and Gisippus, suppressing his emotion, mingles with the guests. At length the affianced pair move on to the bridal. At this point Macready lingered behind, sank upon a bench, and, as the music grew fainter, took off his chaplet, gazed on it wistfully, mournfully; then, with bowed head, let it fall, with a sigh. The wreath seemed to drop on the grave of his illusions.

My next recollection is of an opposite kind; it is that of his towering, scornful attitude, as Spinola, in "Nina Sforza," when, in the fifth act, with foot and sword, he turned over the limbs of the prostrate rival—his house's foe—whose despair and ruin he had accomplished. The intense malignity of the action last named excited the opposition of the pit, but it was true to the hereditary hatred of the character, which, with its duplicity, had been superbly rendered throughout.

Amongst the sources of this artist's inspiration, was that reverential and religious sentiment to

which so many pages of his diary bear witness—
a sentiment which, in poetical natures, begets a
deep sense of the supernatural. Macready had
evidently felt deeply the strange contrasts of
human life—its mournful transiency, and its
persistent love; its seal of mortality, and its
far-extending dreams; the darkness, without revelation, that engirds it, and the yearning, dim, but
ennobling, that points to a lot higher than its
apparent one. Thus, the "Out, out, brief candle!"
of Macbeth; Hamlet's fascinated awe before the
form that, "in complete steel, revisited the
glimpses of the moon," and his baffled conjecture
as to the "undiscovered country;" the solemn
farewell of Brutus to Cassius—

> "If we do meet again, why, we shall smile;
> If not, why then this parting was well made;"

—all these took from Macready's lips and look a
pathetic awe that penetrated and subdued the
hearer. Again, the closing lines of Richelieu,
now regrettably omitted—

> "No; let us own that there is One, above,
> Who sways the harmonious mysteries of the world
> Far better than prime ministers. So ends it,"

were delivered by him, on the first night, with a submissive reverence in striking contrast with his recent bearing as the proud and victorious minister.

In general, he may be said to have excelled in characters and situations where intellect and passion set off each other, as in Lear, rather than in those in which passion largely predominated —in the satire which springs from embittered feeling and in emotional thought, especially when it touches upon mystery and speculation. Hence much of the excellence of his Hamlet. He was at home in finesse and strategy, and in all that involved intellectual gladiatorship, as in Iago and Richelieu. Combativeness in any aspect had a charm for him. Thus his finest act in "Macbeth" was the last, in which the usurper is at bay. He was seldom more effective than in characters of forlorn pride, where the dignity or haughtiness of the man has to pierce through his mean fortunes, as in Werner. In portraying the domestic affections, he shone more as the father than as the lover or the husband. He was not, to my thinking, at his best in characters chiefly contemplative, like Jacques.   On rare occasions he was liable, as in parts of "Macbeth," to suppress impulse by over-elaboration of design. His transitional contrasts of voice, though at times very telling, were often artificial.   His delivery, though most clear and expressive in passages of emotion, was occasionally dragging and spasmodic—a defect probably owing to his advancing asthma; while, to miss none of his peculiarities, he had, in moments of repose, a monotonous proneness to standing in the same posture—one knee, a little bent, before the other.

Among those contemporaries in tragedy with whom I had a chance of comparing him—I was too young to see Edmund Kean or John Kemble —he was *facile princeps.* Neither Charles Kemble nor Charles Kean approached him in imagination or—until the latter left ideal for photographic art —in breadth of execution.*   In both respects Vandenhoff was no less his inferior.   Where his

* In the latter respect Charles Kean's Hamlet was an exception.

way was clear, this last performer had decisive-
ness of outline and force of style; but he lacked
Macready's subtlety and refinement. In these
respects, Butler, who had, undoubtedly, passion
and physical power, was far behind him. Phelps,
after his *début* in London, had, to a great extent,
founded himself upon Macready, and in his tragic
impersonations, with a few exceptions—Hamlet
and Othello, for instance—followed him closely
and often impressively, though wanting something
of his vigour. As to Edmund Kean, though
unable to speak of him from personal knowledge,
I cannot doubt from general testimony, that, in
the exhibition of passion, he was a more inspired
actor than Macready. That wild agony of Othello,
that ever flies from, and still encounters love;
Richard's fiendish cunning and heartlessness, and
his desperate energy of will in the fight where he
" enacted more wonders than a man;" Shylock's
alternations of grief and revenge, as the thought
of his daughter's flight and the hope of Antonio's
ruin seize him by turns,—these, by all accounts,
received from Kean that sudden and terrible

illumination which made Coleridge liken its effect to " reading Shakspere by flashes of lightning." I should not, therefore, hesitate to acknowledge Edmund Kean's superiority to any male performer of his time, since so absolutely to identify himself—if only in certain scenes— with the passions of a human being as to reproduce their most vital manifestations, is, so far, not only to represent, but to *be*, the man.

Yet a sharp line of division between such men as the elder Kean and Macready should be avoided. In harmony of design, and in purely intellectual qualifications generally, the latter had evidently the advantage; while in characters that touched some secret of his own personality, such as Richelieu or Werner, Macready must have approached the spontaneous and life-like intensity of Kean. Regarding, in addition to his wide command of emotion, the depth of his conceptions, the clearness of his outlines, his width of range, his suggestive imagination, and his power of giving to feelings and ideas striking expression in outward form, Macready, whether

compared with his contemporaries or his predecessors, may probably be ranked as the most
intellectual of British actors.   His death took
place in April, 1873, at the age of eighty.

CHAPTER IV.

MR. CHARLES KEMBLE.

A summer evening at the West End, in the season of 1835—
Charles Kemble's Hamlet, at the Haymarket—Cast of the
tragedy—Charles Kemble's appearance and manner—
Description of his Hamlet—His return to the stage in 1840,
by command of Her Majesty—Account of his Mercutio
in " Romeo and Juliet "—His readings at Willis's Rooms,
in 1844—Account of his Faulconbridge in " King John,"
and his reading of that play generally—Presence of the
Queen Dowager—Personal acquaintance with Charles
Kemble—Various fireside readings—Shylock—Richard
the Third—His tragic recitations generally—Resolution
not to attempt John Kemble's parts, with the exception
of Hamlet, till his brother retired—Contrast of Charles
Kemble's style with that of Macready, and (by report) of
the elder Kean—His private readings or recitations in
comedy—A gentleman of the old school in private—Dignity
of his manner and appearance—His conversation generally
serious, with occasional passages of humour—Anecdote
of his brother John—Dispute as to the intelligence of a
popular actor—A test-prologue written for his recitation—
The prologue in question—Mr. Kemble's deafness and
habit of making his confidences aloud—Anecdotes illus-
trative of this—His Epicurean tastes—Talk on the drama
—Suggestion of plots—A domestic story—The reign of
Henry the Second—Mr. David Roberts, R.A.—Mexico and
Montezuma—General estimate of C. Kemble as an actor—

Leigh Hunt's testimony on his retirement—His minuteness
of treatment often unfavourable to passion—Mrs. Siddons
on his Jaffier—General admiration of his Mark Antony—
John Oxenford on the consistency of his characterization,
instanced in Charles Surface—Charles Kemble's death, at
the age of seventy-nine.

AN evening in the summer of 1835 still lives
distinctly in my memory. It was the height of
the season, and when, between five and six o'clock,
I found myself in Piccadilly, opposite the Green
Park (having probably made my way to this
point from the grand old trees of Kensington
Gardens), the road was still crowded with lines
of carriages and equestrians bound to or returning
from Hyde Park. To a lad's eye the scene
was, of course, enchanting. How delightful the
fresh green of the trees, the brightness of the
evening, the effects of sunlight on harness or
emblazoned panel, or the glimpse of grace and
beauty as some fair Amazon dashed by. Then,
on nearing Regent Street, how brilliant the shops
with their glittering windows, where more than
the treasures of an Eastern bazaar were displayed.
These, with the shops of Regent Street itself, had
probably offered me many temptations to linger,

to say nothing of an episodic seduction in the shape of the Burlington Arcade, with its cool, mysterious shade, its treasures of French nick-nacks, its fascinations in haberdashery, its imitation jewellery, and its autographed likenesses of reigning celebrities in opera and ballet. At any rate, it was more than half-past six when I sauntered down the Haymarket. The carriages at the box entrance of the theatre were discharging their occupants, the crowd at the pit had already entered. Charles Kemble was to play Hamlet.

I had, doubtless, previously been aware of this, but, most likely because the actor's fame had been chiefly associated with elegant comedy, the announcement of his Hamlet had inspired me with no especial interest. At the door of the theatre, however, the thought seized me that he was the brother of Siddons, and of that John Kemble whose portrait in Hamlet, by Lawrence, had filled me with many regrets that I had never seen the original. To see Charles Kemble in Hamlet, would be to see, in tragedy, the last

of the old Kemble trio, who, though falling short
in public estimation of his brother and still more
renowned sister, was now their sole male heir and
representative—of one blood with them, so to
speak, in art as well as in life.*

These considerations determined me to witness
the performance. So I passed, by the familiar
door that had often tempted me, into the pit.
Soon the overture ceased, and the curtain rose.
Mrs. Glover was the Queen, Mr. Strickland,
Polonius, Mr. Cooper, the Ghost, and Miss Taylor
(afterwards Mrs. Walter Lacy), Ophelia.

When at length the King, Queen, Hamlet,
and the Court had entered, I felt at once, even
before a sound had issued from the lips of the
melancholy Prince, that in some essential points
my best expectations would be realized. Though
surrounded by good and accomplished actors,
there was in Charles Kemble's look, attitude,
and movement, a charm which, if sad, was

* Years later, on her return to the stage, I witnessed the
representations of his daughter (then Mrs. Butler), who so
well maintained the honours of her line.

so noble and full of repose as to distinguish him from his associates. He was then sixty, and of too massive a presence for his character; but he well counterfeited the suavity and dignity, if not the form and features, of princely youth. His step was stately without being pompous; it had the stateliness of one "to the manner born." When at length he spoke, the perfect modulation of his tones, except occasionally when reaching to a high note (in passion he more than once "piped"), was enchanting. Study, of course, there was in all this, perhaps over-study, though the art of concealing art had, in a great measure, been mastered. I was, however, then too young to be minutely critical,* and surrendered myself with delight to the harmony of the representation. I had never imagined there could be so much charm in words as mere sounds. Next, I was caught by a graceful, pensive idling with those quibbles of the brain in which Hamlet first

* Of course, with respect to Mr. Charles Kemble, and every other performer treated of in my series, I record my early judgments only so far as they have been confirmed and matured by experience.

indulges, that made them seem tricks of fence to ward off approach to his deeper nature. Though they had their touch of causticity, they were thrown off with an air of courtly ease and respect widely different from the intense and scornful significance employed by some actors, who have thus disclosed, at the very outset of the play, Hamlet's loathing for the King. Charles Kemble's fine instinct taught him the unseemliness of launching bitter sarcasms at Claudius before his courtiers. The subdued and delicate irony of his manner might be understood by those whose guilt gave the key to it. To the rest it was the mere humour of the moment, or play upon words. When the Court breaks up and Hamlet is left alone, the soliloquy beginning—

"Oh, that this too, too solid flesh would melt!"

I have since more than once heard rendered with greater bitterness, with more passionate denunciation of the Queen's inconstancy, with a fiercer recoil from the King, but never, I think, with so much pathetic beauty. There was, of course, indignation, but the predominant note was that of melancholy. You heard a wail over human instability, conveyed by a music of delivery which, skilfully varied in its tones, insinuated, rather than forced its way, and made sorrow lovely :—

> " Why, she would hang on him,
> As if increase of appetite had grown
> By what it fed on ! And yet, within a month,—
> Let me not think on't ;—Frailty, thy name is woman ! "

These last words seemed to float away in a very melody of sadness. The fitful and wilder grief that preceded them had sunk into a sigh. While unable at that time to recognize the art which produced this effect, I was deeply conscious of the effect itself. Beauty of treatment, indeed (as contrasted with what is commonly known as power of treatment, though beauty has, of course, its own power), was the feature of the performance. In Hamlet's apostrophe to the Ghost, what beauty of attitude, of tones, which, though subdued and awe-struck, yet found scope for variety. When Horatio and Marcellus would fain restrain him from following the spectre, what grace mingled with the energy of his

struggles, how picturesque was his figure, how
fraught with filial trust and reverence! There
was about him an air of elevation and trust in
his spiritual visitant when he broke from his
companions, which seemed to speak him of a
different and higher nature—as one who had
kinship with supernatural life which they might
not comprehend. The house sat breathless to
see him glide off after his father's spirit, which
magnetically and irresistibly drew him.   To
criticise fully a representation almost embarrass-
ingly rich in delicate and subtle detail, would
be impossible within the limits of this notice.
Passing, then, to his scene with Ophelia, of which
I yet recall the charm—the melancholy, tender
portrayal of a noble soul's distrust, striving with
its love, overcome by it, then reasserting itself
to the close in despair that yet idolized, in
irresistible but mournful upbraidings, blended
and harmonized with fond though vain yearnings
—at the risk of being charged with fine writing,
which every writer nowadays incurs, who
introduces an image from nature into criticism,

I will venture to say that this scene vividly suggested to me a shore at ebb-tide, now bare, now for a moment revisited, even flooded, by the returning wave, which, as it once more recedes, chimes its own plaintive, lingering farewell.

I had not seen "Hamlet" performed before, so that I could not then contrast Charles Kemble's rendering with any other. But, from larger experience, I am bound to say that the play-scene was not given with all the breadth and fire of which it is capable. The under-meanings, however, in the answers to the King and Queen could scarcely have been better conveyed; they were polished, but keen as arrows; while for those fierce and ringing tones of exultation which I heard later from Macready, when the King and Queen hurry from the stage, was substituted a conflict of indignation with grief, which, aided by the actor's grace of delivery and princely bearing, captivated rather than excited the house. His manner subsequently of rebuking the spies was unsurpassed by any I have witnessed. His sarcasms, though given incisively, were so free from violence, and his disdain had such lofty quietude, and such a suggestion of melancholy at the worldliness and insincerity of men, as to reconcile the displeasure of the Prince with elevation both of manner and feeling.

In the closet-scene with his mother, grief and filial tenderness prevailed, perhaps unduly, over the sternness which, however restrained, should still, I think, be in the ascendant; but the noble passages with which the scene abounds gave rare opportunities for the display of an elocution so finished that its art seemed nature. In the scene at Ophelia's grave—though it lacked the overmastering impulse of Macready—the same excellence of elocution was exhibited with great effect ; but what I liked still better in later years (when I heard Charles Kemble *read* "Hamlet") was the tender beauty of the churchyard scene, and his vein of wandering reverie when he followed the quaint, half-humorous speculations of the part with such nice perception as never to disturb the prevailing gravity which they relieved. He was, indeed, a proficient in the display of graceful melancholy, and in the art of enhancing its effect by momentary reliefs of fancy. In the fifth act, his manner of rallying from weighty cares to accommodate himself to the fantastic levities of Osric, his perfect, most musical delivery of the meditative passages to Horatio; subsequently, his "gentle" bearing in the fencing scene with Laertes —the smiling, subdued grace of one only conscious of "the yoke of inauspicious stars," and the tender beauty of his dying,—fitly and softly led to the sleep which "rounded" his princely life.

He may be said to have realized those aspects of the character—its pervading grace, with its contrasts of impetuosity and inaction, of pensiveness and passion, of amiability and irony, all harmonized and made lifelike—which, a few years since, were described by an accomplished critic,* when noticing Mr. Edwin Booth, in language worthy of Hazlitt.

* Mr. Charles Dunphie, who, in his original poems, his felicitous renderings of English into Latin verse, and in several volumes of original essays, has shown not only rare refinement, humour, and keen perception, but a sympathy, under the veil of irony, with right and goodness, which are no less calculated to delight than to attach his readers.

In depth of conception, and in power of rendering, Charles Kemble's Hamlet was inferior to Macready's, which, on the other hand, it excelled in the qualities that endear and charm. As I left the theatre and walked thoughtfully home, it seemed to me as if Hamlet's death had something in common with the night into which the sweet day had merged—a lingering twilight, with the soft mournfulness and tender repose that enchant more than brightness. Hamlet, indeed, was the one Shaksperian character in tragedy in which the excellence of the actor was unanimously admitted. I fancy, however, that he conceived himself to be, above all things, a tragedian; though accident had led him to seek distinction chiefly in comedy. One night, many years after the performance I have just chronicled, he had been reading at my house some scenes from " Richard the Third." Laying aside the book, he observed, in answer to our thanks, " The fame of my brother John in tragedy caused me for long to avoid trespassing upon his ground. To give up Hamlet, however, would have been a sacrifice beyond me."

When, after his retirement, he returned to the
stage for a few nights, in 1840, by command of
Her Majesty, I had the pleasure of witnessing
his Mercutio. Anderson was the Romeo, Miss
Emmeline Montague, the Juliet, Mrs. C. Jones—
a good actress of the Mrs. Glover type, though
much her inferior in subtlety of characterization—
the Nurse.

The spontaneousness of Charles Kemble's
Mercutio struck his audience at once. The art
that conceals art had done its work to perfection.
Besides that ease and distinction which set him
apart, even from actors conventionally graceful
and spirited, there was in Kemble that fresh-
ness which arises when an actor seems to speak
from the impulse of the moment, and when
his utterances are apparently as fresh to himself as to the listener. Thus in the delivery
of the speech describing Queen Mab, the first
line—

"Oh, then, I see, Queen Mab hath been with you,"

was uttered without a touch of formal rhetoric
or *pose*—by no means as a prelude to a set descrip-

tion, but as a simple, whimsical thought springing from mere buoyancy of heart. The thought uttered, you saw that it gave birth to another equally unpremeditated—

> "She is the fairies' midwife, and she comes
> In shape no bigger than an agate stone;"

until, pursuing the image, he had described her journey—

> "Athwart men's noses as they lie asleep."

Then came another sudden burst of fancy, born of the first, gaining fresh strength and impetus in its course, till the speaker abandoned himself to the brilliant and thronging illustrations which, amidst all their rapidity and fire, never lost the simple and spontaneous grace of nature in which they took rise. Mercutio's overflow of life, with its keen, restless enjoyment, was embodied with infectious spirit. There was no gall. If he was betrayed into a duel of words with Tybalt, it was even more by the love of excitement than by enmity; if he was betrayed into the indulgence of ridicule, it was the spirit of mirthful humour that overcame him. I have seen Mer-

cutios derisively cruel in their banter of the
Nurse. With Charles Kemble it was the sport
of the encounter that drew him on. He assumed
a grave, though somewhat exaggerated, courtesy
towards the " ancient lady," as if to mask his
ridicule from her, while enhancing it towards
his comrades. It was only as the jest wore to
its close that his enjoyment overmastered him,
and showed him as a " saucy merchant" to the
offended domestic. It was less malice than the
same keen love of excitement that prompted
him to quarrel. Even in his last encounter
with Tybalt, the crowning provocation was the
imagined wound that his friend's honour had
received by his " dishonourable submission." It
was, again, this full-blooded impulse that angered
him with the elaborate and tutored fencing and
affected airs of Tybalt—" a villain that fights by
the book of arithmetic."

No description can well convey the force and
the varied significance which the comedian gave
to the scene in which Mercutio is slain. How
startling was the former's change of tone after

he deemed Romeo disgraced by his forbearance
with Tybalt!   No more the reckless light-hearted
aptness for the stimulant of quarrel, but the
stern, swift scorn, the lightning-like retaliation of
one whose heart has been pierced, whose person
and cause have been humiliated in his friend.
Scarcely has Tybalt parried the furious thrust,
when Romeo's intervention gives him his chance,
and Mercutio has his mortal wound.   " I am
hurt," he exclaims, at first scarcely realizing
his disaster; then, feeling its deadly effect, " A
plague o' both the houses !—I am sped : "—with
a sudden self-upbraiding, as if he asked why he
had let senseless feuds come between him and
the exulting joy of life.   And yet, soon after
this, with a quaint, comic touch of expression,
that said, the jade, Fate, *will* play men such
tricks, " Ay, ay, a scratch, a scratch; marry,
'tis enough !"   How fine was it, next, to note
the *bonhomie*, the old love of jest struggling
with, and for a moment subduing, the pains of
death, in the answer to Romeo's encouragement
—" No, 'tis not so deep as a well, nor so wide

as a church door; but it is enough. . . . Ask
for me to-morrow, and you shall find me a grave
man."

Here, having achieved this quip, there was a
bright, though quickly fading smile. He was
still the Mercutio of old—the gay, rash, loyal,
boon-companion. It was a smile to call up tears,
it conjured up so much of youth and the merry
past, while it was well-contrasted and kept
within reality by the brief techiness, still not
unmixed with humour, that succeeded—"What!
a dog, a rat, a mouse, a cat, to scratch a man to
death!"—and by the reproof to Romeo for his
fatal coming between—a reproof nobly and pathe-
tically redeemed by the loving courtesy with
which he held out his hand to him, a moment
after, in token of full forgiveness—a point which
was, I believe, original with Charles Kemble, and
which has since become an acting tradition of
the character. Then there came a deep, wistful
expression into his face, reminding you of Romeo's
strange avowal to the Nurse—I am not sure
that it is spoken on the stage—that he was "one

whom God had made himself to mar "—and that there were higher possibilities in the Mercutio of this brief, bright, tragic story, than had ever come to light; but it is too late, said the look; let us wind up with a jest, though it be a grim one—"A plague o' both your houses!"

Such was the impression I have retained of this noble performance, though, as in the case of Hamlet, it is not easy to say how far the subsequent effects of private or public readings and of conversation may have entered into and matured my first acquaintance with it. My *general* estimate of it, however, was the same from the beginning.

Hamlet and Mercutio were the only characters in which I saw Mr. Charles Kemble on the stage. I afterwards heard him read, at Willis's Rooms, part of a series of plays, which included several of his chief Shaksperian impersonations. These were "Hamlet," "King John," "As You Like It," "King Henry IV.," Part I., "Julius Cæsar," "The Merchant of Venice," "Macbeth," "Romeo and Juliet," and "King Richard III."

In this list, though it included my favourite,
" Hamlet," no play had more attraction for me
than "King John," which contained Faulconbridge
—one of Kemble's most celebrated characters.
He had evidently modelled his conception of the
part upon the fact that Faulconbridge was the
son of Richard the " Lion-hearted." As this actor
portráyed him, he might have well stood for
Richard himself, with the addition, perhaps, of a
dashing carelessness and license springing from
the consciousness that his illegitimacy had at
once given him an illustrious father, and yet left
him free from all-bonds of kindred, save those he
imposed upon himself. The intrepidity, the love
of danger and frolic, the occasional penetration
and sagacity of Richard, and his martial bearing
(with, besides, the untaught grace and freedom
of a barbarian chief), were all embodied in this
Faulconbridge, who had an air of unbounded
enjoyment of life, which reflected King Richard's
love of adventure even in excess.

It is hard to convey an impression, to those
who have not seen him, of his delivery of the

dialogue—hard to express the wide difference
between his Faulconbridge and the renderings
of other actors, who have delivered the text
with spirit and just appreciation, and yet fallen
so far short of Charles Kemble as to put comparison out of the question. The secret of his
superiority lay, perhaps, in the fulness of life
which seemed to radiate from him—to make
war a gay pastime, diplomacy a play of wit,
and to clothe worldliness itself with a glow of
bright, genial satire. Thus the celebrated speech
on "commodity," the raillery of Austria, and
the sagacious counsel to England and France to
unite against the defiant city of Angiers, were
given with zest and ardour that were resistlessly
contagious. This impersonation, in a word,
seemed to blend the spirit of Mercutio with
those of the warrior and the statesman. His
Constance had the great merit of harmonizing
the invectives of the afflicted mother with the
dignity of her high station. Except in the
hands of a fine artist, Constance is apt to
become either too sentimental or too shrewish.

His King John abounded in minute and skilful
touches, the great scene with Hubert exhibiting
the advances of the tempter with the nicest
gradations; but he did not bring home to me,
as Macready did, the descent of the Plantagenet
into the assassin.   This, like most of his readings,
was distinguished by a stateliness of expression
peculiar to the Kembles, which I have also
seen exhibited in the powerful and intellectual
performances of his daughter, Mrs. Fanny Kemble.
The series of readings attracted audiences which
included much that was most refined and intellectual in the London of that day.   On the
night of "King John," the simultaneous rising
of the company greeted the entrance of a personage equally loved and revered, Adelaide, the
Queen Dowager.

In 1848, many years after witnessing Charles
Kemble's Hamlet at the Haymarket, I had
the pleasure of knowing him personally.   He
would occasionally gratify me and my family,
and perhaps a chosen friend or two, by reading
scenes from his principal characters at my own

fireside. His selections were sometimes grave
or tragic. He read, or rather, recited, various
scenes of "Shylock" and of "Richard the Third,"
not only with the nice and finished detail and
varied delivery of which he was always master,
but with abundance of fire, the lack of which
had at times been urged against the male
Kembles. The first soliloquy of Richard, when
Duke of Gloucester, touching the defects of his
person, he declaimed with a bitterness of irony
which brought them into the strongest relief as
motives of character. In this opening soliloquy,
he urged, Shakspere meant to give the key-note
of Richard's nature, and to make his deformity,
acting upon a sensitive spirit, the source of his
misanthropy and remorselessness. He showed,
too, remarkable physical energy, though it must,
of course, be granted that a degree of power
very telling in a drawing-room might be far
less so on the stage.

This remark is called for because it has
been alleged that his voice was unequal to the
demand of passion. As to the possession of

mental qualifications for tragedy, these social readings or recitals furnished ample proof. They were the more startling because, with the exception of his Hamlet, Charles Kemble's fame rested upon his successes in legitimate comedy.

In his tragic recitations the dignity of the Kembles fully asserted itself. His style in passion was uniformly lofty. There was variety, indeed—a nice discrimination of emotional changes relieving each other; but it was a variety confined within the limits of what may be called heroic delivery, seldom or never a marked transition from it to colloquial realism. The manner, maintained at the height of the feeling, made no such appeals to the many as did Macready and, according to report, Edmund Kean, by those familiar touches which, at times, set before an audience the individual rather than the typical man. I am not praising Charles Kemble for this habitual loftiness in tragedy. There are times when abrupt changes, failing, confused utterance— touches of realistic infirmity, in a word—convey passion even by their partial inadequacy to express it. It may, however, be said that the heroic school somewhat atones for what it misses by its charm of elevation, while its disciples are generally free from those extravagant contrasts between the ideal and the familiar which is the besetting weakness of realists. To "raise a mortal to the skies" has never, in modern times, been so popular an attempt in art as to "draw an angel down;" but the poet has justly implied that almost equal praise is due to each kind of effort.

As to comedy, his rendering of such scenes as those between Orlando and Rosalind, and Benedick and Beatrice, mingled so happily refinement and delicacy with mirth and spirit, that the mental palate delighted in the selectness of the treat. It was the *grand vin* of comedy, while in sally and repartee there was the nicest precision and point, which yet seemed spontaneous, and a vein of light but ceremonious courtesy in the strife which suggested the grace of accomplished fencers as well as the glitter of the foils.

In society Mr. Charles Kemble was a model
of the gentleman of the old school. His bow,
though it might now be called formal, was stately
and impressive. His dignity of manner and his
tall figure, somewhat massive in his later years,
gave him eminently that quality which is called
" presence," and which we somehow connect more
closely with a bygone period than with our own.
It seemed a wrong to Mr. Charles Kemble's person
that he did not, off the stage, wear knee-breeches,
silk stockings, and diamond buckles, and that he
had survived the time of powdered hair. His
conversation was generally grave, but he delighted
to hear or relate a good anecdote or story, and,
on such occasions, displayed the hearty enjoyment
of humour which had done so much for him as
a comedian. As an instance, I give the following anecdote which he related one day after
dinner, touching his brother John.

John Kemble, he said, was generally supposed
to be a grave and rather austere man, but he
had, in fact, real appreciation of fun. A favourite
brother-actor had one day been dining with him,

and talk of old times had wrought John to
such a pitch of hospitality that he was moved
to produce a bottle of rare port, which he had
so much valued that he could seldom bear to
diminish his stock by drinking it. He did this
port—which had, of course, a particular seal—the
honour of going in quest of it himself. In due
time he emerged from the cellar into the dining-
room, with a bottle of the precious liquid, bearing,
apparently, the identifying seal. The wine did
not, of course, undergo the profanation of decant-
ing, but the two glasses were solemnly filled
from the black bottle. The contents being sipped,
there was, of course, that brief, decorous silence
which the criticism of a noble vintage demanded.
The guest at length observed that it was truly
a remarkable wine, and had a flavour all its own.
The host assented, but fancied, at the same time,
it didn't quite tally with the port in question,
and, though by the seal it must have been the
same, had not the smoothness he expected. The
guest civilly answered that it had a great deal of
life and fine colour, and, holding his glass to the

light, speculated as to whether its peculiar sweetness came from its extreme age. This conjecture
John Kemble, whose palate, perhaps, lacked its
usual fineness of discrimination, did not feel called
upon to discuss; but he owned the " sweetness "
was surprising, and that he greatly missed the
" smoothness." Then a suspicion—fast deepening—dawned on him that there might have been
a mistake. He at length admitted that he could
hardly have brought up the port he went in
search of. His guest, however, who was rapidly
improving his acquaintance with it, maintained
that it was capital stuff. The cautious tragedian,
jealous for the honour of his port, confessed that
the drink before them was not bad, but declared
that it was not the wine he had promised; then
more boldly asserted that, in his opinion, it was
not wine at all. A portion of dark pulp, perhaps,
floating with the beverage into his glass, had
helped him to recollect that his cellar had
lately received the addition of some few bottles
of a *liqueur*. "Why, it's CHERRY BRANDY!" he
exclaimed. This point Charles Kemble made

with all the force of a climax in comedy. It was afterwards discovered that the seals of the port and those of the *liqueur* were identical in colour—a circumstance which had led to the mistake.

John Kemble's companion, on this occasion, was an actor who had held an important position in the theatres both of Drury Lane and Covent Garden. At the former theatre, indeed, he had more than once been the substitute for Edmund Kean, when that actor was unable or unwilling to appear; and he had, in particular, so satisfactorily acquitted himself in the part of Othello, that those in power (Drury Lane was then, I think, under control of the Committee) determined to give him prominence, and thus convey a hint to Kean that they were less dependent upon his genius than he supposed.

The belief entertained of the substitute's adequacy was, however, warmly combated by two friends of the authorities, who contended that the actor's success as Othello was purely exceptional, and due to his close study of Kean's effects. They eventually offered, by way of testing the actor's mental capacity, to write a prologue for him to study, which, though a mere tissue of nonsense, should impose upon him by mere grandiosity of style. The challenge was accepted, the prologue written and confided to the actor, who was delighted with it and eager to deliver it. I do not give the name of this performer, because I have formed a much higher estimate of him than that of his two satirists. The anecdote was told me, as absolutely true, by Mr. W. J. Fox, who also furnished me with a copy of the prologue in question. It runs thus :—

"When Grecian splendour, unadorned by art,
Confirmed the Theban Oracle—in part;
When Genius walked digestive o'er the scene,
In meagre mystery of unletter'd mien;
When man first saw, with an inverted eye,
The tearful breath of purple panoply,—
'Twas then the Muse, with adamantine grace,
Replied, prophetic, from her Pythian base,
And Roscius bent his Macedonian knee
Before the squadrons of Melpomene.

"But mighty Shakspere, whose salacious fire
Waved high his banner o'er the marble choir,

Spurned the base trammels of despotic Jove,
And taught the stern Persepolis to love.
In fancy cradled, like some Northern light,
That westward gilds an oriental night,
Tearing with ruthless hands the sacred root
Of "man's first disobedience and the fruit"—
So waked our bard that histrionic lore
Which Siddons suckled, but which Garrick bore.

" ' Lo, the poor Indian, whose untutored mind'
Through freedom's mists beholds—what's left behind,
Whose ebon limbs those gory bonds entwine—
The heavy, hempen, equinoctial line—
Mutely exclaims and, supplicating, bends;—
' The lovely young Lavinia once had friends.'
So let our author, whose enamelled hopes,
Exfoliate to-night such classic tropes,
Through this, his tragedy, those laurels share
Which Drake and Wickliff both were proud to wear,
And take his chaplet loud from British hands,
As Cato died and Trajan's column stands."

"I have been assured," said Mr. Fox, "that
the actor in question was delighted with the
prologue, and much resented its being withdrawn
before the production of a new play."

At the period of my acquaintanceship with
Mr. Charles Kemble, the deafness from which
he had for some time suffered was become considerable. It had the effect—very frequent in
such cases—of deceiving him occasionally into

the belief that he was speaking in a confidential whisper, when he was really speaking at the top of his voice. This misconception of its range led at times to results which would have been amusing but for the fear that the knowledge of them might have pained him. One night, when he was reading to us, Mrs. Crowe, authoress of "The Night-side of Nature," and of various poems and dramas, chanced to be one of our guests. She showed great delight in his readings, and made herself in every way amiable to him, exerting herself also to meet his infirmity, by speaking in a loud tone on whatever subjects interested him. In the course of the evening he withdrew me to a little distance from the circle, and imparted in stentorian tones an impression which he meant to convey in the most private manner. "What an agreeable and highly intelligent woman," he shouted, "Mrs. Crowe is!" It is almost needless to say that the recipient of this unaddressed tribute was delighted with it, and that, in common with the rest of us, she showed her sense of it only by a smile, quickly suppressed, and unobserved by the eulogist.

The following is an instance, on a wider scale, of the amusing perplexities which sometimes arose from Mr. Kemble's deafness, and his inaccurate perception of the tones he made use of. He had been much impressed by the abilities of a young actress, who afterwards rose to the highest rank in her profession. On being introduced to her his interest increased, and the Nestor of dramatic art gave to the neophyte all the advantages which his brilliant talents and long experience could supply. One of the leaders of society was, through the influence of a friend, won over to the cause of the young performer. With a view of promoting her interests, Lady —— gave a *soirée dramatique* to guests who were, in most cases, representatives of what was then most celebrated or select in the life of the metropolis. The entertainment of the evening was the reading of "Hamlet" by the actress in question. Charles Kemble was present, and it chanced that I sat by his side. His *protégée*—she might almost have been called his pupil—had on the previous evening been reading in public at one of the chief provincial towns. She had, consequently, arrived a good deal fatigued in London only a few hours before the time fixed for Lady ——'s *soirée*. Not unnaturally, at the opening of the reading, her voice was rather feeble, and her manner and expression lacked something of their habitual animation. Charles Kemble was quick to perceive that the lady was wanting in her usual force, and to express his regret and dissatisfaction in accents which were heard by all present, though he fully believed that he was speaking either in unnoticed asides, or imparting his concern to me in the most guarded undertones. "Can you hear her?" was his first high-pitched inquiry; "I can hardly catch a word!" As the reading proceeded, his mortification and the utterance of it became still more emphatic. "Oh, she's so inanimate; she's not doing herself justice! She's injuring herself. I can't tell you how sorry I am; they won't have the faintest idea of her!" It was in vain that I strove to

arrest him, first by silence, then by glances and
gestures. These latter, intended for warnings,
he took simply as signs of acquiescence in his
complaints, and as provocations to their repetition. At length, an intimate friend of our
entertainer was dispatched to me, with an urgent
request that I would apprise Mr. Kemble of the
effect he was producing. To do this, without
exciting general attention, was, on account of
his deafness, a difficult task. To induce him to
leave the room, and then to explain matters to
him as delicately as the case would permit,
seemed the only practicable course. In order
to effect this, I made signs of being overcome
by heat, even to faintness, which soon attracted
his attention. The kind old gentleman soon
proposed that we should leave the room, and
offered his arm to support me. Having quitted
the drawing-room, I threw myself on a chair
in the refreshment-room which adjoined, and
counterfeited a gradual recovery from brief in-
disposition. This point being gained, it seemed
well to turn the conversation upon the reading

of the night, and to observe, in answer to my
companion's renewed lamentations upon that
subject, that the reader, besides suffering from
fatigue, might perhaps have felt a little dis-
couraged by the expression of his disappointment.
"But how could she guess that?" he asked. I
pointed out that her ear was accustomed to his
voice, and that it was just possible some of his
unfavourable comments might have reached her.
"What!" he exclaimed in consternation; "you
don't mean that what I said could have been
heard by any one but you?" I permitted myself
to remark that his interest in the matter had led
him now and then to raise his voice, and I
repeated the conjecture that his brief criticisms
might once or twice have reached the subject of
them. "Oh, I trust not, I trust not!" he cried
earnestly. "I will take care to make no further
observation." I now did my best to lessen his
apprehensions, and he returned to the drawing-
room, I fully hope, with the impression that his
kind concern for me had been his only motive
for leaving it. The heroine of the night was by

this time in full possession of her genius, and, at the close of "Hamlet," deserved and received the warm plaudits and congratulations of the veteran actor, as well as those of the general company.

Charles Kemble had nice and delicate taste in matters of the palate as well as of the intellect. The little dinners at which I assisted, though composed of few dishes, generally included something *recherché*. I once caused him severe mortification by eating a morsel of preserved ginger at the beginning of dessert. "I told you," he said in a grieved and reproachful tone, "that I was about to give you one of the finest clarets, in my opinion, ever tasted, and now you have utterly disqualified yourself for appreciating it."

On one of these pleasant evenings he overflowed with dramatic suggestions, and gave me the outline of an effective plot, laid in former days, in which a young Swiss should marry a girl of foreign extraction, and then, quitting his own country for hers, enter the army of his new home (probably Austria), in which his services should be engaged against his native Switzerland, and thus—an actual, but at first unintentional, traitor —fall into the hands of his father, who should be commandant of a military post on the part of the Swiss. The complications and struggles which this position involved smacked of the "high Roman fashion" of Cato and Lucius Junius Brutus, and of that toga-heroism which the comedian had probably admired in his stately brother. Charles Kemble himself, I believe, in a play, original or adapted, called "The Point of Honour," had delineated a dramatic conflict on lines similar to, though not identical with, those of the plot just described. He also dwelt with great fervour upon the opportunities which the reign of our second Henry offered to a dramatist, with its combination of striking figures—the sagacious Henry himself; his insubordinate sons, Henry, Richard, and Geoffrey; John, who disgraced his descent; the scheming and bold Queen Eleanor, and the hapless Rosamond. On no poetic field, however—except, perhaps, that of the forsaken epic—could such thronging personages and such great events have been adequately displayed. The late Mr. David Roberts, R.A., who was one of our small group on the night referred to, zealousy recommended· the story of Montezuma for tragic treatment. It was pleasant to note the glow in the actor's eyes as Mr. Roberts referred to the stirring incidents connected with Montezuma's life, and to the grand scenic effects which a tale of ancient Mexico would yield. These had, no doubt, appealed strongly to the architectural painter as a noble frame for dramatic action.

One of my latest glimpses of Charles Kemble was due to meeting him one summer day in Great Portland Street, with an open volume, which he had been perusing, in his hand. On my arresting him, he showed me the volume with a gentle smile, and with some remark on its suitability to his years. It was a well-known devotional work —I think, the " Imitation of Christ."

Charles Kemble's retirement happened so soon after I became a playgoer, that, as already stated,

I have had to found my impressions of him on two performances on the stage—those of Hamlet and Mercutio — on a few public and private readings, and on conversations. It is not, however, too much-to affirm that, in his later day, he stood alone as·a legitimate comedian. "Where now," writes Leigh Hunt, on Kemble's retirement, "shall we seek the high Roman fashion of look and .gesture and attitude? Where shall old chivalry retain her living image, and high thoughts, seated in a heart of courtesy,' have adequate expression. Where shall the indignant honesty of a young patriot spirit 'show fiery off'? Whither shall we look for gentlemanly mirth, for gallant ease; for delicate raillery, and gay, glittering enterprise?" In a notice written long before, Hunt praises him as being perhaps, in his "complaining softness," the best of theatrical lovers, were it not for his occasional languor. As to this latter defect, though I saw no trace of it in his Hamlet or Mercutio, it has so often been attributed to him that it probably existed.

That he was relatively unsuccessful in the display of broad and intense passion, is to be accounted for not only by want of physique, but by the minuteness of his style. I have heard him give so many reasons for particular renderings of certain passages in Shakspere, that his notes on the text, if printed, would probably have surpassed it in bulk. Tragedy, as a rule, requires the strong and swift impulse of leading ideas, and the almost unconscious absorption of all minor suggestions into a massive whole. Yet this minuteness was scarcely out of place in the meditative Hamlet, his presentment of whom, though far from being the most powerful, was the most touching and picturesque that I have seen. He had great sensibility, if not overwhelming passion. In one of her letters Mrs. Siddons * avowed her preference for his Jaffier to that of John Kemble, speaking of the latter as being too "cold and formal" in this part, and "without sensibilities sufficient acute for a lover," though admitting his superiority in characters of a sterner kind. From

* John Payne Collier's "An Old Man's Diary."

private as well as public report, it would seem
that Charles Kemble's Mark Antony was one of
his very finest parts, and that his address to
the citizens over Cæsar's body, from its first dis-
claimer of complaint against Brutus, his following
insinuation of Cæsar's virtues, and his apparent
reluctance to read the will which made the
Romans his heirs, down to the grand final effect
—when public indignation had been aroused—
of unveiling Cæsar's body, and appealing to the
crowd for retribution, was an absolute triumph
of skilful, varied, and passionate elocution. As
an instance of the actor's sense of consistency,
that fine critic, John Oxenford, observed that
when the house came to the redeeming points of
Charles Surface, it had been fully prepared for
them by previous indications of the spendthrift's
better nature. This sense of consistency was,
doubtless, habitual with Kemble. An actor of
rare and varied accomplishment is, perhaps, the
phrase which best sums up his claim to admiration—the accomplishment which springs from
quick and sympathetic intelligence, and from a

natural sense of grace and harmony applied and
developed by unremitting labour. This celebrated
comedian had reached his seventy-ninth year at
the time of his death, which took place in
November, 1854.

CHAPTER V.

MR. WILLIAM FARREN, THE ELDER.

Difficulty of replacing him in various characters—His son heir to some of his traditions—Lord Ogleby and Sir Peter Teazle belong to a relatively new era in comedy—The man of fashion from the reign of Charles the Second to that of George the Third—Account of Farren's Sir Peter Teazle—A vein of indulgent cynicism characteristic both of his Sir Peter and his Lord Ogleby — Account of the latter—His Malvolio—His Sir Anthony Absolute—Want of robustness and heartiness—A painter of well-bred people, with their vanities, and other foibles, and redeeming qualities—Excellent in the pathos attaching to mental or bodily infirmities—His best known characters but few —His Bertrand in "The Minister and the Mercer"—His Michael Perrin in "Secret Service," in 1834—The latter piece revived at Covent Garden in 1840—His Michael Perrin described —His performance at the Olympic, under Madame Vestris, in 1837 and 1838—His acting in "Sons and Systems," and in "The Court of Old Fritz"—His Old Parr at the Haymarket, in 1843—His chief excellence in characters of mental.or bodily infirmity—A touch of the morbid necessary to his pathos—His persuasion that he could act tragedy—His attempt at Shylock—His fine discrimination as to expression in acting—Instance of this— His personal appearance—His death.

AMONGST the great actors of the century who are gone from us, there is, perhaps, none whom

it would be so difficult to replace as the late
William Farren. We have, indeed, in the son
who bears his name, a sterling actor, who inherits
some of his traditions and accomplishments; but
the individualities of the two men are distinct,
and the plain, frank manners of our own day
have, very naturally, had their effect on the style
of the present artist. In the mean time, tragic
actors, melodramatic actors, eccentric comedians,
have disappeared, and found successors apparently
to the public content; but the old beau of George
the Third's reign, with the formal characters in
some points akin to him of previous times, took, in
many respects, a long leave of the stage when the
Lord Ogleby, the Sir Peter Teazle, and the Malvolio
of the elder Farren last retired at the wing.

The two former characters belonged to a new
era in comedy. Each differs widely from the
previous type, which had its original in the man
of fashion under Charles the Second. If, on the
whole, a mere libertine, that personage brought to
his love of pleasure a dashing spirit of gallantry
and adventure, for which he was, in some measure,

indebted to the changes of his fortunes. With
one who had known, while yet young, defeat,
exile, and sudden restoration to a splendid court,
life was at fever heat, and the stage showed it.
In a generation or two the romance connected
with the Restoration had greatly subsided. Intrigue, become deliberate, had lost its impulsiveness. The beau, young or old, of that period
was still a wit, but no longer a knight-errant.
After the death of Queen Anne ensued a period
of utter grossness in morals. Vice in high
places, shorn even of wit, looked ugly enough
to produce a reaction towards high-breeding
and decorum. At the accession of good King
George the Third this reaction had already set
in, and, in spite of some excesses in this reign,
was strengthened by the influence of the Court.
The fine gentleman of the time was known by the
disciplined restraint of his emotions and passions,
the plausibility of his language, his formal courtesy, and his minute observance of the punctilios
of etiquette. Gallantry, politeness, and good taste
revived, though they had lost their old spon-

taneity. They were, however, *de rigueur*, as much the external attributes of a gentleman as his lace ruffles or his *chapeau-bras*. The code of honour still existed in all its stringency; but, on the whole, owing to the suppression of natural impulse, existence itself was become a sort of carefully acted comedy. Love stopped short at sentiment and taste, displeasure showed itself by chilling politeness, or, now and then, perhaps, with the old, by a pardonable lapse into testiness. Such was the generation of which two elderly specimens (one furnished by the senior Colman and Garrick, the other by Sheridan) will always be associated with the late William Farren, no less than with his distinguished predecessor, Thomas King. Graphic as is the Sir Peter Teazle of the dramatist, but half of his individuality can be gathered from the written page. In Farren, the unmistakable air of refinement, the dry, quiet enunciation, which added more force to epigram than the most studied declamation could have given; in the scenes with Lady Teazle, the sense of provocation, generally tempered by the

courtesy of a well-bred man to a woman, even
though his wife; the uxorious admiration, oddly
mingled with annoyance, which her brilliant
sallies called forth,—these were felicities of expression which, though suggested by the dramatist,
implied on the actor's part a power of translating
mental ideas into the forms of actual life that was
scarcely short of invention.   Among other subtle-
ties of Farren's performance was the excitement
which now and then contrasted with his habitual
efforts at self-restraint—a display produced neither
by Lady Teazle's recklessness nor by her seeming
heartlessness, but by the raillery which sometimes
made him look absurd.   Thus, his anger was far
less provoked by her suggestion that it would be
obliging in him to make her an early widow, than
by her quotation from that "forward, impertinent
gipsy," Cousin Sophy, who had described him as
"a stiff, peevish old bachelor."   A man of Sir
Peter's type can forgive wrong far more easily
than ridicule.   Farren's touches of extreme irritability when exposed to the latter, set this trait
in admirable relief.

No qualified comedian fails in so capital a situation as that of the "screen scene." For Farren it was, of course, a triumph. One special felicity of his acting deserves, however, to be singled out. I refer to his manner when Joseph Surface, to shield himself from a still graver discovery, pretends. to Sir Peter that he has an intrigue with "a little milliner," who is then behind the screen. I have seen Sir Peters—"and heard others praise them"—who greeted this confession with such explosions of boisterous laughter, that it was clear they had seen nothing in it but drollery. Farren, while fully bringing out what was ludicrous in the position, never forgot the trust Sir Peter had so long placed in the man of moral sentiments. The comedian's air of bewilderment and incredulity, his tickled laugh, at first half smothered out of respect to Joseph, and breaking out in aside indulgences, were as true to the character as they were taking in effect. When Joseph quits the room, and Sir Peter disclosed the secret to Charles, the actor's mirth was naturally undisguised. Yet it was never coarse; it never lost refinement or *finesse*; it was the mirth of a somewhat worn man of society, who finds one of his few piquant diversions in contrasting the set proprieties of outward decorum with the frailties which they affect to disguise. A vein of tolerant cynicism, indeed, is the natural product of an age in which the extreme emphasis thrown upon forms will suggest the discrepancy between them and the qualities they should express. Such cynics, however, have their moods of generosity, since, unless they had an ideal standard of good to which they sometimes conformed, they would less perceive the contrast between forms and realities. Thus, both Sir Peter and Lord Ogleby are at the same time satirical and good-natured. Farren's excellence in the latter character has been attested by Leigh Hunt and Hazlitt, no less than by more recent critics. And what a test character it is for a comedian! What a mixture of shrewdness and infatuated self-complacency, of causticity and courtesy, of puerile affectation and manly judgment, of selfishness and chivalry!

To say that Farren realized and harmonized all those aspects, is in effect to say that he was one of the greatest of comedians. He possessed to perfection the *nuances* of expression, apprehended with the finest delicacy the effect of semitones. To indicate to the audience his delight at his valet's flattery, while he laughs at it, or rebukes it with an air of sincerity; to tolerate the tediousness and bad taste of the vulgar Sterling with a genuine urbanity, which, nevertheless, a lad in the gallery knew to be the disguise of a martyr; to touch the acme of senile absurdity in his wooing of Fanny, and yet to afford through it a glimpse of the knightly feeling which, in his bitter disappointment, afterwards makes him her friend and protector,—these were the achievements of Farren in one of the most elaborate characters in modern comedy. His very appearance in the part was a dramatic effect. In the studied and cautious walk, even in the listless fingers, there was a gleam of the decayed beau, as there was in the character itself a gleam of decayed chivalry.

Not only in showing the marks of social position did this actor excel. He could represent admirably the dispositions and manners of those who covet and ape it; he could assume equally the graceful *nonchalance* of my lord, and the importance and minute ceremoniousness of the major-domo. In personations of the latter kind, as in Malvolio, he would exhibit a delightfully humorous imitation of some rare and subtle quality in true breeding. In many Malvolios the leading feature is contemptuous superiority; in Mr. Farren's it was lofty condescension. He despised the coarse world around him, but he was for the most part affably tolerant to it, as a man who knew the graces, and "practised behaviour to his own shadow in the sun," could afford to be. In characters like Sir Anthony Absolute, in the downright, choleric, but good-hearted stage-fathers of the old school, he was excellent in their impatience, fault-finding, and petulance, but wanted heartiness in their better qualities. There was not a touch of "John Bullism" in his nature. To paint

with subtle insight, and with just, delicate, sure
touches, the vanity, the self-love, the inconsistency, and now and then the redeeming good-
feeling of worldly, well-bred people, and occasionally the credulous faith of simple, guileless
people, were his special functions. Yet the
cynicism from which this capacity springs has
its pathetic side also, and Farren could move one
to tears in such characters as the deceived
Michael Perrin in " Secret Service," or a Grandfather Whitehead, where life itself is touched
with the irony of fate, and second childishness
counterfeits the first in the thoughtless glee,
the doting fondness, and the hysterical passion
of age.

The most widely-known characters of this
comedian are, considering the length of his
career, comparatively few. The cause of this
was probably their frequent repetition. But
the parts in which he deserved to be remembered
would make a long catalogue. In 1834 he made
a great impression at Drury Lane, in a piece
from Scribe, entitled " The Minister and the

Mercer," in which he personated Bertrand, a
scheming diplomatist. He was still more successful in Michael Perrin, in "Secret Service,"
a piece also adapted from the French, and
produced in the same year. Michael Perrin
became one of his stock parts. It was revived
at Covent Gardén, under the management of
Madame Vestris, in 1840. The simple, guileless
bearing of Farren, as the *ci-devant* curé (who is
betrayed, through his affections, to promote unconsciously a political intrigue), his grief when
he learns that his beloved niece has concealed
her poverty and sold one of her trinkets for his
support, his artless joy when he finds himself
able to earn money, and his indignant protest—
all the more powerful because contrasted with the
curé's sweetness of nature—when he learns that
he has been used as a spy, were admirable features
in a performance as consistent as it was impressive. In 1837–8, at the Olympic, where he
succeeded Liston, Farren's acting in "The Country
Squire" and "Naval Engagements" is spoken of
with special praise. To his forcible but delicate

power in dramatic portraiture in "Sons and
Systems" and "The Court of Old Fritz," both
produced at the same time, in 1838, I can
personally testify. In the former piece he played
the part of a father whose theory of training is
that of stern and unrelaxing discipline. To this
character is opposed that of his sister, whose rule
is one of unbounded indulgence. The sister, a
widow, was, by the way, capitally represented
by Mrs. Orger. The systems of both brother and
sister prove equal failures, the sons making their
escape, and marrying in defiance of their parents.
Upon these latter the effects of filial rebellion
are different. The severe doctrinaire father
becomes benevolent and forgiving, the indulgent
mother irascible, and for a time relentless. As
the sharp disciplinarian, with unlimited faith in
his system, Farren's vigour and self-complacency
were admirably assumed, yet with such a touch
of exaggeration, and such an endeavour to justify
his system, that one felt it to be rather the result
of a mistaken theory than of a harsh disposition.
Accordingly, when, after the frustration of his

scheme, he changes under the wiles of his daughter-in-law, disguised as a lad, into a forgiving old man, and inhales with ill-concealed delight the incense offered by the adroit youngster, the transformation seemed as natural as possible, while the phase of pleased senility was as life-like as had been that of the paternal martinet. One capital effect was Farren's amusement at the change in his sister, while decrying her new severity with a self-satisfaction that drolly condemned his former self. Mrs. Nisbett, it may be observed, acted the part of the disguised bride, who wins over the old man. All was prettily and cleverly done, but the part was scarcely one of importance. In the "Court of Old Fritz," Frederick the Great and Voltaire are the chief personages. Both were represented by Farren, who in these delineations gave one more proof that he was an actor who could play not only a range of parts suited to his own personality, but that he could throw himself with success into widely different individualities. No characters could have been more unlike than

that of the brusque soldier-king and that of the
easy and imperturbable wit and cynic; but in
which of these he was the more lifelike, the
objective actor left as a moot-point to the public.
His Old Parr, too, produced at the Haymarket in
1843, well deserves a word, if only for the felicity
with which two phases of old age seem to have
been discriminated. Already a centenarian when
he first appears, Parr still retains activity and
cheerfulness. He is a little garrulous—the only
mental sign of his very advanced age. When the
curtain again rises, nearly thirty years have been
added to his existence. He has yielded to the
infirmities which a term of life prolonged beyond
all modern precedent has entailed. His frame is
bent, his gait tottering, his memory ruined, the
aims of life all but gone, but with them the
cares also. His second childhood, with its innocent diversions, its wandering chat with a lad in
his service, its momentary anxious inspection
of flowers and attempts to name them, its beginning once more to spell out life by the alphabet
—no personation could have been more subtle

or more directly pathetic by the very absence of pain.

It is curious that Farren's excellence seems to have been confined to parts in which infirmity, mental or bodily, was a special trait. In the elderly and uxorious husband, the dilapidated gallant; in the unruffled nonchalance of a sceptic like Voltaire, or the irritable authoritativeness of Frederick the Great; in parts where old age lapsed into the extreme sensibility or the oblivious placidity of second childhood, as in Grandfather Whitehead or Old Parr, or in the credulous unworldliness of Michael Perrin—he was truly admirable; but it is indicative of his mental bias that he could not play, or, at all events, did not choose to play, the hearty, genial Englishman, full of spirit and feeling, and free from peculiarities. He could be pathetic—most pathetic; but there mingled a touch of the morbid in the pathos that suited him. As already hinted, he seemed to the writer a theatrical cynic, who, in portraying the wanderings of men from a mental ideal and a just equipoise of character, sometimes infused into his characters moving or redeeming touches of the ideal itself which had been violated, or of the healthy judgment which had been impaired.

Farren's belief that he could act legitimate tragedy, his appearance and failure in Shylock, for instance, is well known. In poetical passion he could scarcely have succeeded, for the sceptical penetration of the satirist is at war with the enthusiasm that tragedy requires. Yet he could be deeply moved by the enthusiasm of other actors. I recall, once at rehearsal, an instance of his fine perception of the shades of expression. An actress, justly celebrated, had thrown great intensity into the utterance of wounded and indignant love. "What would you say," asked Farren, "to taking that speech just a key lower?" He then recited the passage after his own conception, and all present felt that it had gained in dignity and pathos by the repressed emotion of his delivery.

With his tall form, his full lip, and quiet, unspeculative eye, there was little in Mr. Farren's

appearance off the stage to denote his genius
as a comedian, except in those rare moments
when, interested in talk, it was suggested by his
then mobile and placid face.   His death took
place in September, 1861, at the age of seventy-
five.

CHAPTER VI.

MR. AND MRS. CHARLES KEAN.

The latter part of Charles Kean's career the most notable,
    though his reappearance in Hamlet, at Drury Lane, in
    1838, a great success—Account of this performance—
    Charles Kean less successful in other Shaksperian cha-
    racters—Imitations of his father adopted in 1838—After-
    wards abandoned—Effect of this change—His Macbeth
    in 1849—His Romeo—His Richard the Third—This
    character ranked next to his Hamlet in Shaksperian
    plays — Reasons for his superiority in Hamlet — Per-
    sonal acquaintance with Mr. and Mrs. Charles Kean—
    Favourable first impressions of them—Their generous
    appreciation of dramatic work—They appear, in 1849, at
    the Haymarket, in the author's tragedy entitled " Strath-
    more "—Mr. Kean's performance in this play—Some
    difference of view between him and the author—Mr. and
    Mrs. Charles Kean at rehearsal—Her solicitude for him
    —Their appearance in " The Wife's Secret "—Mr. George
    Lovell—Journey of the writer and a friend with Charles
    Kean to Brighton—A delicate discussion on the way with
    respect to Phelps and Sadler's Wells—Peace secured—
    An amicable dinner—Change in Kean's style of acting
    soon after entering with Keeley on management of the
    Princess's Theatre, in 1850—More original hitherto in
    comedy than tragedy—His Master Ford—His Benedick—
    His Mephistopheles in " Faust and Marguerite "—The
    change in his acting foreshadowed in his comedy—First
    exemplified in serious drama in " The Templar," by Mr.

Selous—His acting in "Anne Blake"—He appears in
"Louis the Eleventh," in the "Corsican Brothers," and
in "Pauline"—He reads to the author various scenes
from "Louis the Eleventh," some time before its production—Great impression produced—A triumph confidently predicted—Account of his performance—Rises to
genius in this and other character parts—Account of his
Louis the Eleventh—This his greatest achievement—Mr.
Henry Irving in the same part—Charles Kean's visit to
Plessy-les-Tours—His Wolsey—His Richard the Second—
Spectacular and archæological revivals—Danger of excess
in these directions—Charles Kean in private—His forgivable egoism—His *bonhomie*, humour, love of fun, and
winning avowal of his weaknesses—His sly raillery of Mrs.
Kean on her susceptibility—Decline of taste for legitimacy
—A melancholy pledge—Quarrel with a dramatic author—
The alleged price of listening to a story—*Ex parte* statement as to the way commissions were obtained from him—
Mrs. Kean's sympathy with him—Hereditary genius—His
father's fame, in his opinion, detrimental to him—His
strong desire to find his opinions adopted and his side in
a quarrel espoused—This illustrated by his difference with
Douglas Jerrold—Causes of this—Censure of Mrs. Kean's
acting by a critic—Charles Kean's strange method of
resenting this, and annoyance with the author for disapproving of his retaliation—His avowed objection to
impartial criticism. The model of a theatrical notice—
Hears a detailed eulogy of his wife's acting in a particular
play—Demands the speaker's opinion at equal length on
his own acting—Resents the notion that a man ought not
to be praised to his face—His expedient for meeting this
objection—A last interview with him—A glimpse of him,
during illness, at Scarborough—His death—Brief summary
of his claims, professional and private.

MUCH that is most noticeable in the career of
Mr. Charles Kean is exclusively connected with

its later period. Had he died or retired before his lesseeship of the Princess's Theatre, in 1850, what was most individual in his acting, and what most distinguished him from the number of fairly intelligent and well-trained tragedians who have their day, and then glide out of recollection, would have hardly been surmised. However, his reappearance in "Hamlet," in January, 1838, at Drury Lane, after a long course of preparation in the provinces, was, it must be owned, a great success—the first he obtained in London. I well remember the excitement with which I read the eulogies of the Press generally upon this performance, and the fervour with which my youthful judgment endorsed them, when, one night shortly after his reappearance, I struggled into the pit. Nor was this impression deadened when, after a lapse of years, I saw the same actor in the same part. He had at that time enriched it with many new details. It is true that his Hamlet was not remarkable for subtlety, nor even definiteness of conception. Whether he

inclined to Goethe's view of the character, or
to any other in particular, could not very easily
have been determined. Psychology in poetic
characters was not yet, at all events, one of
Mr. Kean's strong points. But the grace and
earnestness of his style, the care bestowed upon
the delivery of favourite passages, and the skill,
not always free from artifice, with which certain
effects had been prepared, delighted many who,
if they could secure a varied and brilliant
display of emotion and stage effect, were not
nicely critical as to depth of conception and
harmonies of characterization. Charles Kean's
acting in his first interview with the Ghost
was greatly admired. Awe and filial devotion
could hardly have been more effectively mani-
fested. In addressing the Ghost his tones were
generally hushed and tremulous. It seemed as
if he had felt that mortal sounds were too
gross in so dread and sacred a presence. Yet
there were moments when the majesty of the
apparition seemed to raise and inspire him.
Nothing could have been finer than his tone

of growing confidence and exaltation when he rejoined to the expostulations of his companions—

> " Why, what should be the fear?
> I do not set my life at a pin's fee;
> And for my soul—what should it do to that,
> *Being a thing immortal as itself?* "

Performers of Hamlet are always applauded when they break away from Horatio and Marcellus to follow the Ghost. There is, of course, great opportunity for a telling struggle, and for a striking contrast between the tones Hamlet employs to his companions and those addressed to the Ghost. Charles Kean seldom missed a point where stage effect and true feeling are thus capable of being united. I have never seen an actor who more fully conveyed the feeling that his fate " cried out " to him with tragic vehemence to obey his father's summons; I have never seen a Hamlet whose grief for his father was so pervading, so inwardly gnawing. It surpassed that of either Macready or Charles Kemble, imparting a more sombre character than theirs to the Prince's irony, and a darker colour of present suffering to his indignation. It is not

at all meant that his indignation was softened
by his grief—on the contrary, his self-reproach,
and his invective against the King in the
soliloquy beginning, " Oh, what a rogue and
peasant slave am I!" were amongst his most
passionate and successful explosions—but that,
whereas, with the two other performers named,
grief seemed at this point to have been almost
absorbed in the desire for revenge, in Charles
Kean's case anguish for his father's "taking off"
was as vividly portrayed as if the event had
been of yesterday.   He was very successful in
the scene with Ophelia, the poignancy of his
invective being accompanied by an expression
of such forlorn hopelessness, that his love revealed
itself, not only in spite of, but by means of his
bitterness.   His burst after the play-scene, as
he threw himself on Horatio's neck, "Why, let
the stricken deer go weep!" etc., had a rare
mingling of wild energy and hysterical grief.
In the closet-scene, his denunciation of the King
and of his mother's perfidy was less forcible than
Macready's, probably because, in his expostu-

lations with the Queen, the sense that he was still her son was, under the circumstances, almost unduly apparent. His most effective, but somewhat tricky point, after killing Polonius, of sliding up to the Queen, while, with eyes riveted on her, and a hissing voice, he exclaimed, "Is it the King?" roused frantic applause. These were the salient points of his representation, of which the general characteristics were fervour, grace of bearing, and a pervading melancholy which approached the sentimental.

Apart from his Hamlet, many effects of which had, from an executive point of view, been most thoroughly studied, I was seldom greatly impressed by this actor's performances in Shaksperian tragedy. On the occasion of his reappearance at Drury Lane, he had introduced various imitations of his father, on dismissing which his acting, spite of occasional bursts of vigour, for which he reserved himself, grew comparatively tame. His Macbeth, when I saw it—in 1849, and subsequently—was painstaking, but, on the whole, feeble and colourless. He had freed him-

self in a great degree from the point-making
which at one time beset him; but, in rejecting
theatricality, he had not, except in Hamlet, and
perhaps in Richard the Third, attained tragic
power. It may be that in "Macbeth" he had hus-
banded his resources for the great demands of the
last act, where he showed much physical energy,
carrying the audience away, if I may say so, by
the "pluck" of his acting. It was exciting; but,
for want of skill to distinguish nicely the relation of Macbeth's conflicting qualities with each
other, his rage, his defiance, his recklessness, and
his disgust with life were so many changing
phases to which you had no sufficient key. You
had less the thought of a combat with Fate than
of a bull-fight, and of the brave and frantic
efforts of the tortured animal in the arena. It
should be said, however, that he gave with much
pathos and taste the soliloquy—

> " I have lived long enough: my way of life
> Is fallen into the sear, the yellow leaf; "

and that after the Queen's death, with its melancholy iteration—

" To-morrow, and to-morrow, and to-morrow,
Creeps in this petty pace from day to day."

His Othello, after he discarded the ultra-vehe-
mence of his early style, was on the same level
as his Macbeth, its painstaking inadequacy being
somewhat redeemed by the actor's great knowledge of stage business and effect, though it
presented no sustained display of energy and
abandon, as did his final act in the latter tragedy.

I once saw him act Romeo. He had not the
romance or the chivalrous tenderness of the
lover, but he showed great energy in the scene
of passionate grief with the friar, and in the
scene where Romeo kills Tybalt. His Shylock
was conventional, but fairly effective. In Richard
the Third he was more than conventionally good.
The sardonic, crafty, unscrupulous, and determined Richard lay well within the range of his
conception, while his rendering of it—animated,
and full of variety and contrast—did not greatly
betray his old sin of staginess. If his Richard,
more than any of his Shaksperian performances,
was founded on his father's, it was yet so earnest

and living, one could not but feel that its adopted points had been thoroughly assimilated. His Richard the Third stood next to his Hamlet as a success in tragedy. His superiority to the end, in the latter, may be accounted for partly by the romance of the character itself, with its sensitiveness to impression, its contrasts of aspiration and despondency, tenderness and satire; by those quick transitions of the eventful story which perpetually stimulate the actor; and, lastly, by the fact that his first great success in London had been won in the part, and that he associated with its poetry something of the glow and ardour which attached to his comparatively early and gratifying triumph.

I made the acquaintance of himself and his wife in 1849. Mr. Webster had placed in their hands a tragic play which I had written for the Haymarket Theatre. I called upon them soon afterward, and can remember few first interviews which gave me greater pleasure. . Their simple cordiality and a certain playfulness of allusion on the husband's part to matters in which we

were both interested, while the smiling counte-
nance of his wife spoke her enjoyment of his
humour, made me at home with them at once.
Nor could anything be more frank and generous
than their estimate of the play, in which they
were soon to appear. I may here say that, at
a later period, when Charles Kean became lessee
of a theatre, he and his wife never failed to
express the same open and lively pleasure with
dramatic work that engaged their sympathies;
they never resorted to the poor stratagem of
depreciating what they intended to buy.

In the summer of 1849 Mr. and Mrs. Charles
Kean appeared in my tragedy of " Strathmore,"
which, it may be well to say, has no likeness of
character or plot to a novel which has since been
widely known under the same title. Mrs. Charles
Kean's performance in this play shall be treated
of later. Having studied every detail carefully,
in conjunction with his wife, Mr. Kean won the
warm approval of the press and the public, no
less than that of the author. He threw into
the chief situations an intensity of feeling which

riveted the house. The writer of the piece
differed with him, however, in one point, and
that an important one. The phantoms of old
memories which beset the excited imagination of
Strathmore—after, in pursuance of duty, he has
doomed the father of his betrothed to death—were
meant in the end to be dispelled by his sense of
right and moral necessity. Charles Kean, on the
contrary, abandoned himself to unresisted anguish,
which culminated at the fall of the curtain. He
suggested Orestes pursued by the Furies. "Don't
you think that fine?" said Mrs. Kean, apart,
to the writer, when her husband went through
the scene in question at rehearsal. "Very
intense and effective," was the answer; "but——"
"Oh, do tell him so!" she interrupted; "it will
give him new spirit." "But it's not what I
meant," was the reply; upon which the author's
view was explained to her, and subsequently to
the actor. "I will try to express your view,"
said he; "but I am disappointed that you do not
like mine. What should I make of the situation
if I acted it thus?" He then gave the writer's

conception, but with such tameness and want
of sympathy that the audience would, without
question, have been far less moved by it than by
the previous rendering.　The author held to his
conviction that, if his notion had been sympathetically carried out, still higher effectiveness
would have been secured, as well as truth of idea.
" Oh," cried Mrs. Kean, in an earnest whisper,
" don't thwart him !　I like his way better than
yours ; but, if it were wrong, his heart is in it,
and he will make far more of it than of your way,
which does not seize him."　So far as the effect of
his acting in this particular scene was concerned,
there was truth in this reasoning.　A sort of
compromise between the two views was effected
in theory ; but, in practice, Mr. Kean was always
mastered by his original bias, which is hardly to
be wondered at, as he gained great applause by
following it.　I give this little relation as an
instance of the watchful care to gratify her
husband which Mrs. Kean never failed to evince.

Amongst other plays produced by the Keans
at the Haymarket was the popular and effectively

constructed " Wife's Secret," by the late Mr.
George Lovell, who united to his dramatic gift
such a faculty for business that the Phœnix Life
Assurance Company, of which he was secretary,
testified their sense of his great services by presenting him with his portrait. Mr. Lovell was
the author of " The Provost of Bruges," a tragedy
which Macready persuaded Bunn to produce at
Drury Lane.   Though the piece was abruptly
withdrawn, it was greatly and deservedly applauded, its situations being finely conceived, its
dialogue showing throughout vigour and fancy,
and rising towards the close to great power.
This play was reproduced by Phelps at Sadler's
Wells.   It is one that, with a reviving taste for
the poetic drama, will probably reassert its claims.

" The Wife's Secret," without being a play of
so high a class, afforded many and great opportunities to the performers who represented its
hero and heroine. Of these Mr. and Mrs. Kean
availed themselves with such marked effect, that
the piece remained for years amongst the most
attractive in their *repertoire*.   During what may

be called the period of Charles Kean's first manner, there were few dramas in which he displayed more fervour or achieved greater success.

Shortly before he became co-lessee of the Princess's Theatre with the late Mr. Robert Keeley, I and Mr. A., a friend of mine, met him by chance at London Bridge Station. We were all going to Brighton, and it was at once arranged that we should travel in the same carriage. That which we entered was occupied only by ourselves, and our privacy was uninvaded during the journey. This circumstance, which seemed conducive, by freedom from restraint, to social enjoyment, proved in the result a little unfortunate. My friend A. was almost as impulsive and open-hearted as Kean himself, and, in his willingness to communicate, did not sufficiently weigh the possible effect of his communications. When I had introduced him to Kean, who already knew him by repute, the talk naturally turned upon theatrical matters, and, in particular, upon the prospects of the legitimate drama, which Kean's near enterprise at the Princess's was intended to promote. Then ensued the following dialogue, which, though reported after many years, is substantially accurate throughout :—

"There are, and always have been, difficulties in the way of highest art," observed Kean.

"Yes; the fit audience is too often the few," answered A.; "and the difficulty is still greater where the few are divided."

KEAN. "Excuse me, I don't quite understand. How divided?"

A. "I mean this; whenever the legitimate drama has prospered, there has always been one actor whose supremacy was undoubted, as in your father's case, and, in a less degree, in Macready's."

I began to think we were on delicate ground. Macready's supremacy was hardly a point to be insisted on to a contemporary tragedian. A.'s simple-mindedness and interest in his subject had evidently hid this truth from him.

A. (*continuing*). "However, Macready's engagements in London are likely now to be comparatively short ; but you must prepare yourself, Mr. Kean, for a hard battle with the supporters of Phelps."

KEAN (*after a pause*). "But Mr. Phelps is the manager of a suburban theatre ; our interests are not likely to clash."

A. "Oh, pardon me, he draws to Sadler's Wells intellectual playgoers from all quarters— the West End, the Clubs, and the Inns of Court —and they swear by him."

MYSELF (*trying to effect a diversion*). "You told me, Kean, that you play to-morrow at Brighton. I suppose Mrs. Kean is there ? "

KEAN. "Not yet ; she will follow me."

A. (*charged with interest and information*). "And I am sorry to say, Mr. Kean, that the admirers of Phelps, at Sadler's Wells, are not always generous partisans. Sometimes they assail you openly in the theatre, by shouting out comparisons when Phelps makes a point."

KEAN (*a little restlessly*). "Of course I can't expect to be a favourite with Mr. Phelps's audience."

A. " Perhaps not ; but, still, partisanship should
have limits."

MYSELF (*interrupting*).   " Favourite actors, of
course, have partisans."

A. (*addressing* KEAN). "Why, in the last pantomime at the Wells (I am sure without Phelps's
authority), —— made up for a complete carica-
ture of you, and did all in his power to make you
ridiculous.   Of course, the many roared ; but I
condemned the whole exhibition.   I tell you this
only to show that Phelps has a powerful following
in the public, as well as in the press, and that you
will doubtless have something of a battle to fight
with him."

A faint laugh from Kean, a muttered aside, and
at last this dangerous subject was dismissed.   It
spoke well for his amiability that, on our arrival
at Brighton, he insisted on our dining with
him.   He probably discerned the truth that
A.'s disclosure had flowed from an open and
guileless nature, quite incapable of giving
intentional offence.   Fortunately, the dinner
passed away in cheerful talk and anecdote, with

no recurrence to the disquieting topic of the morning.

From the time that Charles Kean entered, in 1850, upon the management of the Princess's Theatre with Mr. Robert Keeley (who soon after retired), the signs of a broad change in his acting, even in serious pieces, became apparent. In comedy, though he played it comparatively seldom, he showed from the first more original insight than in high tragedy. There was much individuality in both his Master Ford and his Benedick. The former, indeed, was an excellent personation. It abounded in those quaint and realistic touches which he afterwards threw into his serious acting, of which it was to some extent an adumbration; for his second manner in serious drama may be described as a quaint blending of the minute and homely traits and humours with a tragic force, which they kept within the limits of a somewhat grim reality. The mingled agitation, perplexity, and humour of the scene where Master Ford, for his own ends, eggs on Falstaff to tempt his wife, and of subsequent scenes; the

restless aside glances and gestures by which the
actor revealed his jealous pangs; his rage at the
intending seducer, and his shame at himself for
practising a mean stratagem—were so expressed
as to prove at once the reality of his passion,
and provoke irrepressible mirth at the oddity of
its manifestations.

The same minuteness and force of silent expression proved very telling in his Benedick,
which showed a frank, genial enjoyment of jest
and repartee that at once commended it to his
audience.   No part did he invest with so much
eccentric humour, or with so many complex
effects, as his Mephistopheles in "Faust and Marguerite"—a piece taken from a French version of
Goethe's great poem, which ingeniously contrived
to eliminate the poetry.   Kean produced "Faust
and Marguerite" at the Princess's, in 1854.   The
tawdry nature of the piece in general was redeemed
by his acting of Mephistopheles.   The contempt
of this personage for human failings and incon-
sistencies was blended with a sense of so much
amusement at them, and the satirical comments

were uttered with so much dry indulgence, that
the sinister Mephistopheles became far more
diverting than many characters in set comedy.
Now and then, however, there was a revelation of
something terrible in the grotesque individuality
—like the gleam which suddenly comes into the
eye of a playful cat at the sight of a bird—which
made the entire effect unique.

It has already been said that his peculiar
qualities in comedy foreshadowed much of the
coming change in his serious acting. Perhaps
the first example of it was his acting in a
piece entitled "The Templar," written by Mr.
Selous, and produced early under the Kean
and Keeley management of the Princess's. In
this piece Kean had to personate a wronged
man yearning for revenge, but compelled for
awhile to hide his purpose. The "reserved
strength"—to use a later phrase—which he
displayed, the occasional dry colloquialism, and
the tendency to express passion rather by
significant low tones than by exertions of the
voice, were remarked upon by several as a

4

contrast to his former high, declamatory style in tragedy. The delivery of one line—

"The tiger crouches ere he takes his leap,"

produced a great effect by its quiet, ominous concentration. At the end of the play, a keen, if somewhat fastidious critic—the late Mr. G. H. Lewes, no warm admirer of the actor—observed to me, "Charles Kean is changing his style into a natural one. He will convert me yet."

A still more conclusive proof of his new predilection in art was supplied by his acting in the present writer's play of "Anne Blake," produced at the Princess's, in 1852. Though a drama of contemporary life, the incidents and characters were such as demanded the exhibition of strong emotion; and Mr. Kean admirably reconciled this necessity with the tone and habits of modern society. Once or twice, indeed, he seemed to sacrifice the *abandon*, of which he was capable, to a desire to conform to the usages of the drawing-room; though, as the events were more exciting and romantic than those which generally transpire in drawing-rooms, more demonstrative feeling

than is generally found there would have been
allowable, even granting the doctrine—which may
undoubtedly be pushed too far—that the habits
of a period have a despotic right to govern its
emotions. Still, it must be said that the performance in question was one of great excellence,
of admirable keeping, and of a manly, if, at times,
repressed force, which made its way to the heart,
through all the impediments of everyday customs
and attire.

But it was not until the production of Mr.
Boucicault's version of "Louis the Eleventh"
at the Princess's, in 1855, that Charles Kean
set the seal upon what I have called his second
manner in tragedy. This manner, as has been
said, combined the quaintest realism of detail,
sometimes embracing the minutest peculiarities
of a character, with all the heat of passion.
Other indications of this might have been
found in the deadly coolness of his revenge
and hatred in " The Corsican Brothers," and
in the hero of the drama called " Pauline."
In the former it would have been difficult to

surpass the quiet and menacing intensity of
his acting, or, in the latter, the effect of passion
at white heat, strangely enhanced somehow by
the realism of modern costume and the nonchalance of modern manners.   In the duel-
scene of this piece he held the house breathless.
By the conditions of the duel, the result must
be fatal to one of the combatants.   Thus the
silent, concentrated quietude with which Charles
Kean prepared for the encounter ; the way in
which he combined the merciless determination
of fixed hatred with the refined ease and placidity
of the man of society ; the air of calm acquiescence in his fate when he removed from his lips
the blood-stained handkerchief which betrayed his
mortal wound,—all these details, if less ambitious
than those of his acting in tragedy proper, far
surpassed them generally in dramatic suggestiveness, incisive power, and freedom from artifice.

Some time before the production of " Louis the
Eleventh," Charles Kean had recited to me, at his
house in Torrington Square, several of its most
telling scenes, including that memorable passage

in which Louis, while arranging a murder with two
of his creatures, on hearing the *Angelus,* devoutly
takes off his cap, garnished with leaden images
of saints, reverently mutters a prayer, and then
returns to the project of the murder in the identical tone of voice he had used when interrupting
himself.   I well remember my delight at an
effort which, in my opinion, promised to eclipse
all his previous successes, and I was so far carried
away by my admiration as to say this, when,
troubled for a moment, he exclaimed, " Yes ; but
what of Shakspere ? "   Shaksperian characters,
it was agreed, did not fall within the range of
comparison, after which he showed the heartiest
pleasure at my prediction of a signal triumph
—a prediction which it is needless to say was
thoroughly fulfilled when the tragedy was at
length brought out.

Charles Kean's success in Louis the Eleventh
served to prove conclusively that, if he was an
average actor in heroic parts, he was an original
genius in certain character parts—that is, parts
which exhibit various human passions, with a

modification of their expression peculiar to the
person represented. His appearance, as he first
came upon the stage—the askant and furtive
look, the figure bent slightly forward, the slow
and wary step, the hands closely locked—
conveyed at once suspicion and keenness to detect,
and foreshadowed a singularly individual representation. Selfish cunning, unscrupulous and
remorseless meanness—meanness even to abject
fear—were the leading features of the personation;
yet through these penetrated often the habit of
authority, and even, at moments, something that
revealed the royal strain of the house of Valois.
In the first act, the desperate love of life which
prompts Louis to moderate his rage, after the
warning of his physician, his brief relapse, and
his attempt to bring impetuous passion within
such limits of cool malignity as might be safely
indulged, were given with such truth to nature,
and with so admirable an ease of transition, that
deep interest and eager expectation were aroused
before the actor had been many minutes on the
stage. The scene where the King insinuates to

Tristan the murder of Nemours has already been
alluded to. It is enough to add that when, at
the ringing of the *Angelus,* Louis interrupted
himself, and, hat in hand, muttered his prayers
in a hypocritical parenthesis, and, on the bell
ceasing, resumed the suggestion of the murder
in the very tones and words with which he had
broken off, the wonderful picture of wickedness
and dissimulation converted expectation into
fulfilment, and convinced the playgoer that his
gallery of dramatic characters was about to be
enriched by an arresting portrait. So truly was
every following scene realized, that it would be
mere monotony of praise to dwell upon the sick
King's delight with Marthe when she rallied him
upon looking so young and hale ; upon his almost
paternal kindness, not over-emphatic or over-
sweet, to Marie, when he strove to worm from her
the name of her lover to destroy him, while his
face, when averted from her, revealed his craft
and relentlessness ; upon his feigned humility to
the Burgundian envoy, till, hearing of his master's
defeat and death, he gives, with fierce exultation,

the order for his arrest. The scene, however, in which Nemours threatens Louis with instant death, introduced effects so new to the stage in a tragic actor, that it must have special record. First, there was the effort to meet the terrible emergency with submission, conciliation, denial of guilt, and prayers for mercy. Then, as resource after resource failed the threatened man, there rose from him, with frightful iteration, a cry like that of some hunted creature in its extremity— not a natural, pleading cry, however abject, but the scream that speaks of a horrible, purely animal recoil from death. The effect was appalling. In a poetic or heroic character, however criminal, such horror would have been out of place; but in the base nature of Louis, only idealized later by the actual presence of death, it was in keeping with the Dutch literalness, or rather, the grim Hogarthian significance of the entire study. Repulsive, but never to be forgotten, its sudden and terrible fascination for the audience was something like that felt by a wayfarer of old, when lamp or torch on the road abruptly disclosed to him the erect gibbet and its hideous burden. In the last scene, the character of Louis, with its fearful realism, was almost redeemed by Charles Kean into poetry, so vividly did he present the solemnity of death. As the King tottered on to the stage—a crowned spectre, swathed in royal robes—his look caught something of awful dignity from his consciousness of doom; his face bore the seal of mortality. The vain effort to cheat himself into a belief in returning vigour, the spasmodic attempts at action, the greedy clutch at the crown that is passing from him, his terror at the announcement of death struggling with his desire for vengeance on Nemours, the final terror which makes him forego that vengeance, the sense of vanity in all earthly things, and the piteous cry changing into desperate command for the prayers of those around—all these in their detail had no less of imagination than reality. Few more impressive moments of the stage can be recalled than that in which Louis, believed already dead, rises and thrusts his ghastly face between the Dauphin and Marie,

as if to revoke the pardon to Nemours. The
frantic yearning for life and power was, indeed,
so depicted, that the King's death was a relief
from painful but absorbing tension. Awe and
pity pervaded the hushed house. After such
agony, even a wretch like Louis could be pitied.
The play of " Louis the Eleventh," though strong
only in its one central character, gives great
scope to a fine actor. Louis at once became
the great feature of Charles Kean's *répertoire.*
Those who have seen Mr. Irving in the part may
congratulate themselves that it has by no means
passed away with the actor who introduced it
to England, but retains, spite of some points of
difference, its old power and individuality in the
hands of its later representative. I may here
observe that, some time after his appearance in
" Louis the Eleventh," Charles Kean paid a visit
to Plessy-les-Tours, marked by its associations
with that execrable monarch. In one of the
tragedian's letters, I had an interesting account
of the visit in question.

After the performance of Louis, Charles Kean

never went back entirely to his old style, even
when representing poetic characters. His Wolsey,
in " Henry the Eighth," became as individual a
churchman in his way as is a modern ritualist,
while his Richard the Second abounded in those
realistic peculiarities which distinguish men of
kindred nature from each other, rather than in
those ideal qualities which express the general
likeness of men of the same type.   But his
portraiture had now acquired more than conventional accuracy ; it had something of that
poetic truth which is the inmost reality. There
is no great need, however, to dwell on his
spectacular revivals, such as " Sardanapalus,"
" A Midsummer Night's Dream," " Henry the
Eighth," and " Richard the Second," in all of
which pageantry was not only introduced but
obtruded, while in the last work a display
of too minute correctness in armorial bearings,
weapons, and household vessels, made the Stage
an auxiliary to the Museum, and forced it to
combine lessons on archæology with the display
of character and passion. Of course, correctness

and suggestive beauty of illustration are in themselves commendable; but it can surely never be right that accessories should overpower our interest in the actor, who, if he have genius, will often rivet us heart and eye upon himself, so that we forget the accessories. It would be difficult to name the exact point at which spectacle ceases to minister to dramatic effect and begins to impair it. The decision as to this will not be the same with every playgoer, but it will probably be the same with all intelligent audiences, and thus justify or condemn the particular spectacle exhibited.

No subsequent impersonation of Charles Kean showed power so striking and original as that revealed in his Louis the Eleventh. With the remarks on his great acting in this character, my criticism on the actor, therefore, almost ceases.

As a man, notwithstanding the pardonable egoism which he took no pains to disguise, Charles Kean had many qualities that ensured not only esteem but attachment. He was irreproachable in his domestic life, free and open in

his manners, and faithful to his engagements.
When free from the nervous anxiety and sensitiveness which at times troubled him, he showed
a *bonhomie* which was quite charming—quaint
humour, childlike enjoyment of fun, and a
guileless frankness in proclaiming his own weaknesses which utterly disarmed censure. His
generally grave expression, and his guttural and
rather monotonous voice, were obvious dis-
advantages; but now and then they lent a
peculiarly dry effect to his passages of humour,
in the course of, or at the end of which a very
winning smile would perhaps light up the
gravity of his aspect, and reveal his sly enjoyment beneath it. This kind of serious humour
he indulged habitually in private. Mrs. Kean's
quickness of emotion when rehearsing her parts
gave frequent openings for his grave sallies. He
used to rally the writer by complaining that his
wife was more affected by the study of his characters than was good for her spirits. "Marston,"
he exclaimed at a family dinner one day, when
Mrs. Kean was carving, "I fancy you are for

a second slice of mutton.   Please address yourself to me, and I will communicate with my wife.
A request for mutton from you would probably
throw her into tears, and force her to leave the
table."   This was said with a stolidity of manner
that made it doubly waggish, while the gleam in
his eye told how much he relished the pleasantry.

His profits from "The Corsican Brothers" were
far greater than those from any other work he
had produced.   "Ah," said he, with a melancholy
which the monetary success of this piece a good
deal tempered, "the old legitimate drama is fast
dying before these new sensations.   Fill your
glass, and let two old-fashioned actors drink
sympathetically with an old-fashioned dramatist.
Perhaps we shall be the last of our race."

On the same occasion—for trifles had sometimes importance to him—he related with some
glee how he had out-manœuvred a certain dramatic author, who evidently designed to cut him
in the street.   "No, no," said he; "Charles Kean
is not a man to be cut; so I bore down upon
him, said 'How do you do?' and forced a gruff

response, without offering my hand." On my
asking what offence he could have given this
gentleman, he answered, "The offence of telling
him, when he entered my dressing-room some
nights ago, that I was glad to see him, but that
I could not afford to let him *tell me a story.*"
"And you were both on the best terms a short
time since!" said Mrs. Kean, regretfully. This
phrase, "Tell me a story," seemed to need further
explanation; so a full statement followed as
to the disagreement between Kean and his
author. According to this possibly biassed
version of the actor-manager (Kean was then
lessee of the Princess's), he had been surprised
by a demand, on the part of his former friend,
for the price of a drama which had recently
been rejected. The author maintained that the
piece had been written under contract, but this
Kean emphatically denied. "Had any terms
been discussed?" I asked. "None whatever,"
was the reply; "but it was doubtless understood
that if I liked the piece I should give the terms
I had previously paid him." "On what, then,

does he ground his claim for a contract?" "Ah!
there it is," exclaimed the sympathetic wife.
"Like one or two others, he asked Charles to
listen to an anecdote." "Just so," resumed the
manager, with a pathetic sense of his hardships.
"He walked into my room, and, after the usual
greetings, said, 'Kean, shall I tell you a story?
I, of course, knew that 'story' was another
term for 'plot of a play.' I answered that my
arrangements were made for some time, but,
with that explanation, I was always glad to
hear any notions of established authors. He
told the story. I thought it very taking—you
know how well X—— tells a story. 'You like
it, then?' said he. 'Do you like it well enough
to let me set to work upon it?' I referred to
the difficulty mentioned—the pieces I must bring
out previously—but said I should certainly like
to see his drama when completed. It *was* completed—clearly in a hurry. The strong points of
the tale had been so weakened by diffuse talk
and by a poor underplot, that I could scarcely
have believed a dramatic story could have been

so spoiled by a practised writer. I declined the piece as politely as I could, and was then met with the demand to pay for it under my contract. Of course, by saying I should like X—— to set to work, I simply meant that the idea of the piece was worth pursuing. I had no conception that I was committing myself to take it, however it might turn out. X—— has, at all events, taught me this lesson—that it is a very risky thing for a manager to let an author sit opposite to him in his dressing-room and regale him with 'a story.'" I laughed, saying I should take his warning, and henceforth send my stories to him on paper for his acceptance. My impression is that a compromise was afterwards arranged between Kean and the dramatist, and a good understanding in some measure restored.

The conversation turned one day upon hereditary genius. "A man may be very proud of his father's fame," he said; "but in some cases it's about as damaging a legacy as can be left to him. If it had not been for *my* father's fame, I should have made my way with the public

twice as easily.   When I took his view of a
character, it was the fashion with shallow people
to call me an imitator.   On the other hand,
when I took a line specially my own, the cry
was, 'What a difference between Charles Kean
and his father!'"   "Quite true!" exclaimed Mrs.
Kean, with her unfailing wifely devotion.   At
that time, when Charles Kean had not shown
the marked originality he afterwards evinced,
it did not appear to me that his father's renown
had been a serious disadvantage to him.   It
would have been uncourteous to state this view,
so I made some general remark, which I fancied
my host received a little dubiously.   No man
more liked an emphatic assent to his opinions.
He would even take it a little amiss if you did
not espouse his cause vigorously when he chanced
to have a quarrel.   On the occasion of his
difference with Douglas Jerrold, he signified his
intention of sending me his version of the case
so soon as it should be printed.   Perhaps this
announcement drew forth no particularly warm
response from a man who, having already heard

the opposite version, knew that something was to be said on both sides. Subsequently, Mr. Kean stated his grievance—or what he believed to be such—with so much energy, that his companion was obliged to remind him that he was on friendly terms with Douglas Jerrold, whom he frequently met, and for whom he had much esteem. This remark was followed by a gloomy silence and a speedy close of the interview, in which " Good mornings " were exchanged somewhat briefly. A staunch adherent himself, Charles Kean did not greatly relish impartiality in his friends where his own interests were concerned.

The coolness between him and Jerrold was owing to some difference respecting the comedy by the latter, entitled " St. Cupid." At an earlier period, however, than that just referred to, Kean had been a good deal mortified by some expression of Jerrold's. A piece of his had been chosen for the royal theatricals at Windsor. Of these Kean was the manager. Jerrold, who desired to be present at the acting of his piece, had

asked Kean whether this wish could not be grati-
fied.   Kean did not see his way to it, as no
person could be present at these entertainments
without a special invitation or command. " However, Jerrold," said he, " I might possibly take
you under my wing, and you might witness the
piece from the side of the stage." " *Take me
under your wing !* " ejaculated Jerrold, who perhaps suspected an assumption of patronage. " I
can dispense with seeing the piece; but I can't
reconcile myself to seeing it ' under your wing.' "
" And why should he not have gone under my
wing ? " demanded Kean, in bitter resentment at
the implied slight.

Charles Kean fully appreciated the devoted
attachment of his wife, and was almost as sensitive as he would have been in his own case to
any censure of her acting.   On one occasion his
displeasure at such censure showed itself in a
curious and, probably, unique manner.   A certain
dramatic critic, who had often written warmly
of both Mr. and Mrs. Charles Kean, in one particular character so far disapproved of the lady

that he spoke of her acting as "vulgar." Vulgarity was certainly not a fault with which Mrs. Kean could fairly be taxed in general, and the imputation of it to her, perhaps not unnaturally, called forth her husband's indignation. Calling on him one morning, he related to me the offence, and the somewhat droll retaliation to which he had resorted. "I wrote to the critic of the ——," he said, "and requested the favour of an early interview. He came the morning after I wrote. I asked him if he had written the notice in question, which he at once admitted. I then charged him with having insulted Mrs. Kean by calling her vulgar. After a little demur he said he had a perfect right to call her acting vulgar if he thought it so. 'No, no!' I cried"—here Kean turned to me with the vehement desire that he sometimes showed to have his opinion endorsed —"no man has a right to call my wife vulgar, either on or off the stage." After a moment he asked my judgment on the matter. To his obvious annoyance, my answer was, that though I by no means agreed with the writer of the

notice, yet I thought if he honestly, however mis-
takenly, believed that an actress was vulgar, he
had a right to say so. He had a right to say
that a poet or painter was vulgar; why not say
so of an actress? "It was false, and it was
intended for an insult!" cried Kean; "so I simply
said to our critic, 'I shall give you a lesson
against insulting my wife in future.' I got up,
left the room, locked the door from the outside,
apprised the servants, directed them not to go
near the apartment. After some hours I returned,
and gave order for the prisoner's release." I
could not resist a laugh in saying that his conduct
had been quite illegal, and that he had made
himself liable to an action for assault and deten-
tion. "Oh, it was capital fun!" said Kean,
giving way to more impulsive laughter than he
often indulged in. "Depend upon it, the position
was too absurd for him to make it public." The
critic, in his turn, told me the story of his
" durance." "Oh yes, I took it quietly," he said,
with a philosophic smile. "One does not provoke
a madman, but amuses one's self with his antics."

It has already been said, in effect, that, with
the love of distinction which belongs to artists
of all classes, there was mingled in Charles
Kean's case a boy-like openness and *bonhomie*
in admitting, or rather, proclaiming his foibles,
which, far from offending, attracted the listener;
he could not but feel won by a nature which had
no reserves and desired none. On his expressing
dissatisfaction one night with a criticism which
was, on the whole, very favourable, it was suggested to him that a touch of fault-finding, as
showing impartiality, gave added value to a
laudatory notice. " Oh, I hate impartiality ! "
exclaimed the frank actor; " I like the admiration
that carries a man away, and won't let him stop
to think of a few slight and accidental defects."
Not long after this, on a chance-meeting in the
street, he drew from his pocket a daily paper,
which, with a solemn and impressive look, he
put into my hand. The paper contained a well-
written notice of Charles Kean by a friend who
had attained a high position both in law and in
literature. The well-written notice proved to be

a long and elaborate panegyric which, so far as I can remember, was nowhere spoiled for the actor's palate by the hint of a single blemish or defect. "Do read it carefully," said Kean, with earnestness. "That's what *I* call criticism!"

Of the unusual candour of his avowals, an amusing instance occurred one night in his dressing-room. When I entered, the curtain had fallen for some little time upon a play in which Mrs. Kean and himself had been acting. Mr. George Lovell, the dramatist, was about to quit the room as I passed in. "Remember, Lovell— remember," cried Kean, laying more than his accustomed stress upon his "R's," "that Mrs. Kean is in the manager's room. Go to her at once!" Mr. Lovell smiled, exchanged greetings with me, and went out. "I have something good to tell you of our friend Lovell," began Kean, in considerable excitement. I composed myself to listen, and he continued—"Lovell was greatly delighted with my wife in our new piece. In that he resembles all who have seen it; no one knows better than I how well she deserves his praise.

And it was good, downright praise. He went
into the performance, act by act, almost point by
point. After a time I said to myself, 'Nothing
can be more true. I wonder whether what he
has to say of Charles Kean will be as nice?' On
he went—capital praise—praise that showed how
well he understood her. Still no mention of
Charles Kean. 'Oh,' thought I, at length, 'I see;
he will first finish with her, then begin with me.'
He *did* finish with her. 'Lovell,' I said, 'your
opinion of Mrs. Kean delights me.' 'It is quite
sincere,' he answered; and then—what do you
think he did? He held out his hand and said,
'Good night, Kean!' '*Good night!*' I echoed,
astonished; '*good night?* And you have not
uttered a word as to what you think of Charles
Kean in his new part!' 'I think very highly of
him,' he replied. 'Very glad to hear it,' said I.
'Then just be good enough to stay a few minutes
and go a little into the matter.' What do you
think he said to that? He pleaded the d——d
rubbish that he couldn't praise a man to his face.
'Lovell,' I said, 'have no scruples with me. I

act for the very purpose of being praised ; I like
to be praised.   Above all things, I like to be
praised to my face.'   However, he begged to be
excused, since, though he had great admiration
for my acting, he really couldn't express it at
length to *me*.   'Well, Lovell,' I answered, 'Mrs.
Kean is now in the manager's room.   Go to her;
give her your opinion of Charles Kean, act by act,
with the same minuteness with which you have
given him your opinion of her.   She will convey
to me what you are too delicate to express.'
Then you came in.   Stuff—stuff!   Not praise
a man to his face!"   I have heard him more than
once repeat this anecdote to his acquaintances,
with his usual dry enjoyment in relating any
humorous passage in which he had taken part.

After he resigned the management of the
Princess's, I had but few opportunities of meeting
with him.   The last, I think, was at breakfast,
at the Great Western Hotel, Paddington, when
I had the pleasure, after a slight difference, of
renewing cordial relations with him, and of
extending his term in a little drama, which, after

all, he was unable to produce, and which was eventually produced at the Haymarket, under the title of " The Wife's Portrait."

In the autumn of 1866 I chanced to be at Scarborough. The evening before leaving, when passing by one of the hotels—I think the Prince of Wales's—there appeared, framed in one of the windows, a worn, pallid face, with a look of deep, melancholy abstraction. " Charles Kean!" I exclaimed to myself, and prepared to retrace my way and call. But, having heard already that he had been seriously unwell while playing a round of provincial engagements, I thought it better not to disturb him or to bring home to him a grave impression as to his health, even by a card of inquiry. In little more than a year after this his death took place. It occurred in January, 1868, when he had reached his fifty-seventh year.

Reverting to him as an actor, it may be predicted that his Hamlet, with its varied and finished execution, will dwell in the memory of all survivors who have seen it. Many of these will also recall his claims in some other well-known characters already mentioned, to which may be added that of Sir Edmund Mortimer in "The Iron Chest"—a part, it is said, into which he threw much of his father's harrowing intensity in scenes of remorse. But he will undoubtedly be best remembered by his Louis the Eleventh, which, in its fusion with passion of the extreme realism previously almost confined to comedy, formed a new type of acting on the English stage. His friends who are still amongst us will cherish the recollection of a high-principled gentleman, warm in his attachments, generous in extending to others the appreciation he coveted for himself, and gifted with a charm of simple candour that made even his weaknesses endearing.

CHAPTER VII.

MRS. CHARLES KEAN.

Mrs. Charles Kean (then Ellen Tree) in "The Red Mask," at
Drury Lane, in 1834—Her acting in "The Jewess," etc.,
in 1835—The original Clemanthe in Talfourd's "Ion," at
Covent Garden—She subsequently appears as Ion at the
Haymarket—Notice of her performance—Appears, in
1839, at Covent Garden, under the management of Mr.
and Mrs. Charles Mathews, as the Countess in Sheridan
Knowles's "Love"—The run, then extraordinary, of that
piece—Macready's statement as to the then average attrac-
tion of legitimate plays, and as to "The Lady of Lyons"—
Miss Ellen Tree's acting as the Countess—As Ginevra, in
Leigh Hunt's play, "The Legend of Florence," at Covent
Garden, 1840—Leigh Hunt's tribute to her—Appears,
same year, in Knowles's "John of Procida," at Covent
Garden—In 1842 (then Mrs. Charles Kean) appears at the
Haymarket in Knowles's "Rose of Arragon"—Her acting
in the two plays last named—Indifferent as Juliet and
Lady Macbeth—Description of her acting in the latter
—Her Gertrude in "Hamlet," Marthe in "Louis the
Eleventh," Katherine in "Strathmore," and Anne Blake in
the play so called—Brief summary—Personal appearance—
Her death.

MUCH that relates to Mrs. Charles Kean, pro-
fessionally and privately, has already been told

in connection with her husband. Some further particulars respecting her may, however, be stated.

I first saw her in 1834, at Drury Lane, in an opera called "The Red Mask; or, The Council of Three," founded upon Cooper's novel of "The Bravo." Several good English singers were included in the cast, but the character assigned to Miss Ellen Tree (subsequently Mrs. Charles Kean) was one simply for acting. The plot of "The Red Mask" was more dramatic than that of operas in general. Miss Ellen Tree had no great opportunity until late in the piece, but she then availed herself of it with so much pathos and force as to win from her audience the most sympathetic admiration. In Gelsomina—such was the name of her character—she is said to have made a decided advance in public favour. For myself, then a boy in a jacket, the incidents of the opera, and even those of the novel, with which I made acquaintance later, have faded from my mind. I cannot recall the situations which Miss Ellen Tree made so powerful and so touching; but I remember walking home with dim eyes, with her exquisitely feminine and expressive voice still in my ears, and as romantically in love with her as an impressible lad could well be.

A great success is recorded of her in the following year, when she performed, at Drury Lane, the heroine of " The Jewess," a drama adopted by Planché from the original of Scribe. In this drama, it may be mentioned, Mr. Vandenhoff also distinguished himself as the Jew, Eleazar. After "The Red Mask," I saw Ellen Tree as the Witch of the Alps, in Lord Byron's tragedy of " Manfred," which has been noticed in my first chapter.

Miss Ellen Tree was the original Clemanthe in the late Mr. Justice (he was then Serjeant) Talfourd's tragedy of "Ion," when produced at Covent Garden. She performed that character, according to Talfourd himself, with " elegance and pathos." It did not give scope for any great tragic power. On account of an engagement at the Haymarket, Miss Tree was obliged to resign the part, which Miss Helen Faucit consented at a short notice to study, thus leaving the poet fortunate in each of his interpreters.   In the course of her Haymarket engagement, the run of " Ion " having expired at Covent Garden, Miss Ellen Tree reappeared in the tragedy, this time as its hero. After the signal triumph of Macready in the character, her attempt was a bold one. Miss Tree, however, if she had not, in like degree, Macready's power of relieving a part, and his saliency in presenting details, brought very special gifts to her interpretation. Face, form, voice, and simple grace of manner combined to make her externally the ideal of her character, while its purity, nobility, and self-sacrifice, found such sympathetic rendering, that, if I may judge by the experience of my friends and myself, the effect was ennobling no less than touching, while, at the close, the spectator withdrew reverently as after a religious observance.

In 1839 we once more find Ellen Tree appearing at Covent Garden, then under the management of Mr. and Mrs. Charles Mathews (Madame Vestris), in Sheridan Knowles's new play, "Love."

To the amazement of London, the play ran fifty nights—then an extraordinary number for a legitimate piece, although it had been much exceeded in melodrama, as in the case of "Black-eyed Susan." For a new work of higher pre-tension, especially if written in blank verse, twenty nights in the course of the first season was thought quite satisfactory.

I remember Macready observing that, in the days referred to, twelve or fourteen paying houses to a successful legitimate piece were as many as could be reckoned on. Of course, at rare intervals, there were brilliant exceptions. One of these was "The Lady of Lyons," which, to the best of my remembrance, ran about thirty nights in its first season; but, *en revanche*, I heard from the manager's own lips that he played it for the first fortnight to half a pit, and that it would then have been withdrawn had it not been for the author's generosity, which called for unusual exertions on the part of the lessee. These, with the intrinsic attraction of the piece and the dis-closure of Bulwer's name, at length raised the drama into popularity.

To return to Knowles's play and Miss Ellen
Tree. The long run of "Love" may be chiefly
attributed to her acting. Although "Love" has
some strong scenes, the interest is anticipated,
and declines greatly after the third act. Mr.
Anderson, again, though an actor of gallant bearing and some emotional power, had not then
gained such distinction as to make him the hero
of a theatre like Covent Garden; while Madame
Vestris, though she assumed masculine dress, had
no very telling part. The emotional interest of
the story centres in the Countess (Miss Tree's
character), and in Huon the Serf. The former
character, moreover, contains much delicate psychology, and gives fine opportunities for contrast.
These contrasts, indeed, would be too extreme,
did not the dramatist intend to imply the growing
love of the Countess for the serf by the excess
of her scorn in resisting it. The conflict indicated was shown, not too sharply, but with a
harmony of treatment that reconciled and blended
the most opposite effects, both in the opening
scene, where Huon reads to the Countess the

story of a peasant who loved a lady of high degree, and in the hawking scene of the second act, where she stands rooted with terror to see the serf leaning against a tree, while the lightning plays around him, and yet struck dumb, lest she should betray her too great stake in his safety. Nothing could be truer to the strife in her nature than her arrested movement and riveted gaze before the serf is struck, her agonized cry and bound towards him when the event occurs, and the overdone indifference and hysterical levity of her feigned gaiety when she hears that he has only been stunned. In the third act her power of facial expression was put to a severe test. Huon has rejected the contract by which the Duke, her father, seeks to bind him in wedlock to another, and death or the galleys is threatened at the end of an hour, should he still refuse compliance. The Countess, immediately after the departure of the Duke, wrests from Huon the truth of the matter, and, while holding in her hand the contract which, for her sake, he has renounced, has to express

silently the last combat between her pride and
her love, and the triumph of the latter.   The
strife, with all its alternations, could not have
been told so vividly by any language.   The
audience hung suspended on the mute battle-
field of her face, following every turn of the
struggle, and breaking into passionate applause
at the close, though not a word was spoken till
she exclaimed, over-mastered, "Huon, I die!"
Her deep sweetness of manner verged upon
humility when at last she owned her love; yet
there was a dignity and a power of self-govern-
ment about her which revealed the influence of
race.   She was the Countess of the first act,
exalted over her pride.

I missed her personation of Ginevra in Leigh
Hunt's "Legend of Florence," produced at Covent
Garden, in 1840.   The sweetness of her long
forbearance under the taunts of a jealous and
malignant husband, and her pathetic force when
she is at last goaded to resistance, were univer-
sally admired.   Her delivery of the following
was specially extolled:—

> " *Gin.* I scorned you not, and knew not what scorn was,
> Being scarcely past a child, and knowing nothing
> But trusting thoughts and innocent daily habits.
> Oh, could you trust yourself!—But why repeat
> What still is thus repeated, day by day,
> Still ending with the question, ' Why repeat ? '
> [*Rising and moving about.*
> You make the blood at last mount to my brain,
> And tax me past endurance. What have I done,
> Good God! What have I done, that I am thus
> At the mercy of a mystery of tyranny,
> Which from its victim demands every virtue,
> And brings it none ? "

I have heard Leigh Hunt speak enthusiastically of her acting in his play. He betrayed something akin to her own sensibility when he spoke of her bright eyes glistening through tears as she delivered various lines that touched her at rehearsal.

Ellen Tree appeared at Covent Garden the same year, as the heroine of Sheridan Knowles's " John of Procida." At the Haymarket, in 1842, she (then Mrs. Charles Kean) was again enlisted for a play by Knowles, " The Rose of Arragon." " John of Procida " supplied her with no great situation. She had some chances, however, of showing her devotion to her lover and her father, and these she improved with the sympathetic

truth that was her special gift. "John of
Procida" can hardly be ranked amongst its
author's successes; yet its second act is a
remarkable achievement. It consists of a duo-
logue in which no external event takes place,
its breathless interest lying in the revelation of
himself by a patriot-father to a son who lives
in ignorant friendship with the enemies of his
country. In "The Rose of Arragon"—at least, in
its earlier scenes—Mrs. Charles Kean had somewhat better opportunities as Olivia, the peasant
girl who has secretly married the despotic King
of Arragon's son, and warns him of danger,
though, on the discovery of her marriage, he
has caused it to be annulled and banished her
from the Court. The ingenuous earnestness of
her manner when risking her own life to save
that of her stern father-in-law, was one of the
chief effects of the piece. Another was her
resistance to a sensual villain who has her apparently in his power. The situation is certainly
old enough; but the nobility of her bearing, and
the splendid energy of her defiance and detes-

tation, revivified towards its close a story which was gradually become feeble.

Amongst those results which baffle anticipation, and for which it is hard to assign a cause, was the qualified success of Mrs. Charles Kean in Juliet. With her excellence in characters of sweetness and devotion, and her power of passionate expression, one would have said in advance that this was, above all, a part in which she would have triumphed. It proved otherwise. Of course, experience, taste, and, in a degree, sympathetic feeling, veiled her want of vital individuality in the character. The spectator, nevertheless, went away disappointed. Perhaps because Juliet is not, after all, eminently a character of self-sacrifice; perhaps because the performer had concentrated her mind upon the acting difficulties of the character, and striven to master them as isolated effects, rather than by entering into Juliet's nature—she did not carry the audience with her, as she had done in many parts offering meaner opportunities.

It might have been predicted that Mrs. Charles

Kean would scarcely make a striking Lady Macbeth. With her fine intensity of feeling, fervour of exposition, and power to translate herself into various types of life, she could hardly be said to combine imagination in its strictly poetic sense. She loved to seize those traits which bring a character within the range of actual life—no doubt an excellent method generally, though its sole use hardly suits those types which, while essentially true, are too remote and awful for familiar treatment. The intuitive feeling which divines at a glance from a mere external fragment the spirit of the whole, and which rather descends from the spirit to the form, than attains to the spirit through the form—the method of Siddons and Rachel—was probably beyond this fine artist, —at least, in conceptions of mystery or guilt, to which she could not bring the immense aid of her personal sympathy. Hence there was a sort of artificial moderation in her rendering of Lady Macbeth's terrible adjurations. It seemed as though she had doubted that an actual woman could have uttered them, and had therefore striven to give them reality by softening their extravagance. From the hints of one or two mighty phrases, on the other hand, an imagination like that of Mrs. Siddons would, one may conceive, seize the *soul* of the woman, take *that* as the reality, and care little whether the probabilities of actual expression were overpassed or otherwise.

Again, in the great scenes of the first and second acts, an attempt was made to present Lady Macbeth under the two aspects of determined will and wifely fascination; but these phases of the character were alternated rather than fused. Mrs. Kean did not seem to perceive that, to a mind like Macbeth's, vacillating between two principles, resolute will was itself part of the fascination, and that, until his crime was committed, she was glorious to him through the very scorn with which, for his sake, she had denounced his weakness.

She was good, however, in her watchfulness over Macbeth in the banquet-scene, and if her feverishly hurried manner of dismissing the guests and repairing to her husband took something from the evil woman's self-control, it was eloquent of conjugal solicitude. In the melancholy and remorse which set in after the murder, she was also more at home than in certain of the previous scenes. Her grief, however, was too simply tender; her sleep-walking scene had not the abrupt flashes of recollection that reveal the hauntings of conscience; her remorse was like the repentance of a nature which had originally been good.

In her later years she often played Gertrude in "Hamlet." It was one of her most perfect representations. Her air of apprehensive melancholy, born of secret guilt; her looks of wistful yearning, at times suddenly repressed, towards her son; the obvious compulsion she put upon herself, in the closet-scene, so much being at stake, to "lay home" to him his offences; the divining, shown by a quick, averted look, of his terrible impeachment ere it had well begun; the mechanical way in which her one or two phrases of resistance were urged, and her complete breaking down before the consciousness of her guilt and the eye of her son—scarcely left a detail wanting in the impressive conception. Fine as is the character of Gertrude, it is, of course, so dominated by that of Hamlet, that Mrs. Kean probably performed it so often simply for her husband's sake. Another and much stronger instance of the immolation of her professional interests to his own, was her performance of Marthe in "Louis the Eleventh." Yet her life-like rusticity, the blended bashfulness, apprehension, and shrewd resource with which she clothed her French peasant, raised the little sketch into such prominence that it became the second feature of the play. In two plays of the writer's—"Strathmore" and "Anne Blake" —she displayed pathos so subduing, and traits of character so just and arresting, that he cannot dwell upon them without seeming partly to appropriate the praise that was her due. In fairness to her, however, it should be recorded that her enunciation of the words, "No; die!" when, in "Strathmore," she confirmed her lover

in his resolve to accept death rather than false-
hood, not only overpowered the house, but won
from the press some of the rarest tributes ever
paid to an actress.

In sympathetic emotion, as distinguished from
stern and turbulent passions, no feminine artist
of her time surpassed her; in suggestiveness of
detail, no artist but one. Her range was un-
usually large. Mirth and humour came as
naturally to her as self-devotion and tenderness.
Her sense of enjoyment was contagious, and free
from the slightest touch of coarseness. Her
performance of Marthe, just referred to, showed
what she could do in characters of eccentric
humour. I have heard her at rehearsal, in
offering suggestions—which she did with especial
tact—assume the language and the looks of the
various characters so admirably, that she seemed
equally at home in each. The beauty of her fair
oval face, with the expressive eyes, and the nose
slightly aquiline, accompanied with the charm
of her refined and emotional voice, were most
captivating in her youth, and much of their attrac-

tion lasted to the end of her career. Amongst the women of the English stage who have recently passed from us, there is no figure to which I turn with more general admiration or with profounder esteem. She died in the summer of 1880, at the age of seventy-five.

CHAPTER VIII.

MR. BENJAMIN WEBSTER.

First acquaintance with Mr. Webster—"Borough Politics"—
His quarrel with Mr. and Mrs. Charles Mathews—His
habit of confiding differences to others—Called a "good
hater"—Certainly a staunch friend—Of a sensitive disposition—His feeling of comradeship—His resentments not
lasting—His reported challenge to Macready—His fidelity,
as manager, to the interests of his company—Interview
with him — His personal appearance and manner — An
agreement concluded—His badinage—His frankness and
promptness in negotiations—His acting in a little comedy
by the writer—Width of his range—His desire to extend
it—I read to him some scenes of a poetic drama of which
I desired him to play the hero—His pleasure at the proposal and his misgiving—Reasons for it—Variety of his
acting in dramas of real life—Account of his acting in
"The Roused Lion"—Allusion to the excellence of Mrs.
Keeley in the same drama—His acting as Squire Verdon
in "Mind Your Own Business"—His nice balance of
various features of character — This exemplified — His
Richard Pride — His Graves in "Money," Triplet in
"Masks and Faces," Reuben Gwynne in "The Round of
Wrong"—His Tartuffe—Objections to that comedy—His
Jesuit Priest in "Two Loves and a Life"—His Robert
Landry in "The Dead Heart"—Mr. David Fisher in that
drama—Mr. Webster as Penn Holder in "One Touch of
Nature"—His faults—His Petrucchio—His Wildrake in

"The Love Chase"—Dragging delivery in his later years
—His services as a manager—"The Heart and The
World"—Supper after a failure—Dinner to Webster at
Freemasons' Tavern—The Shakspere Committee—Web-
ster's Institutions for actors—His reception in Paris by
Napoleon III.—Mr. Robert Bell—Welcome to Keeley—
Webster's death—His reputation as an actor and in private.

MY personal knowledge of the late Mr. Webster
dates from an early period of 1845, at which
time he was lessee of the Haymarket Theatre.
I had sent him a comic drama, "Borough Politics,"
which will be more fully alluded to when I
have to speak of Mrs. Glover.

In two or three weeks' time I received from
Mr. Webster an ' obliging letter, in which he
ascribed his delay to the embarrassment into
which Mr. and Mrs. Charles Mathews had
thrown him by abruptly leaving the theatre.
He dwelt emphatically upon what he considered
the unjustifiable nature of their conduct, in a tone
that seemed to demand sympathy for himself.
This tendency to repose confidence in one almost
a stranger was, I found afterwards, characteristic
of him, at least, in the vigour of his days. If he
liked you—and he took strong likings—you and

your friends were his friends, and he doubtless expected reciprocity. I have heard him called a good hater and a staunch friend. It was my good fortune to know him only in the latter character. He had now and then a way of beginning a sentence in a tone of great cordiality, and of ending it in a tone of reserve, which seemed, I thought, to belong to a nature at once warm and proud, which was jealous of having its regard surprised. It is probable that, with his sense of good comradeship and his eager disposition to prove himself a true ally, he was exacting as to reciprocity, and retentive of what he conceived to be a slight or a wrong. But his resentments were less enduring than they were said to be. A bitter coldness took place between him and the Keans when they arranged to become co-lessees of the Princess's with Mr. and Mrs. Keeley. To quit his theatre for the purpose of conducting a rival house, very likely appeared to Webster, with his strong cleaving to old fellowship, something like a breach of the decalogue. But if his convictions as to mutual duties were somewhat strained, it is just to say that he obeyed them implicitly, and that, for the sake of past associations, performers were wont to be retained in his theatre long after their salaries exceeded their attractions. With his sensitive character, there is reason to put faith in the report that he once sent a challenge to Macready, who replied that he would be willing to accept it when his correspondent had taken rank as a tragedian by a successful performance of Hamlet. However, it was under Webster's management that Macready's farewell performance took place, the relations between lessee and manager being then most cordial. The former, however, after the sums which he had paid to the tragedian, somewhat resented his speaking at a public dinner of Sadler's Wells, instead of the Haymarket, as the future home of legitimacy. With respect to other little feuds, I believe both those with Mr. and Mrs. Mathews, the Keans, and the Keeleys—if, indeed, the last were ever regarded as *participes criminis*—were eventually composed. Indeed, at the dinner given to

Webster about 1865, Keeley was one of the most interesting figures.

As to myself, an interview followed quickly upon Mr. Webster's letter. I had not before seen him off the stage. He was rather tall, with eyes of a bluish grey, a fresh complexion, a figure slightly tending to corpulence, and an engaging frankness of manner. He at once accepted my terms, and the little piece was produced with a result which, I trust, was not ungratifying to him. A few days later, on being with him in his room, he said, in his rather high-pitched voice, with a sly laugh, "Well, we talked about terms; but I suppose you poets write for fame, and would despise anything so vulgar as a cheque." "And you actors and managers," was my reply, "you, too, doubtless work for fame; but would you be content without salaries or profits?" Seriously, no manager could have been more pleasant to deal with. In my own four or five contracts with him, I never knew him attempt to beat down the price of a piece by depreciation—by remarking, for instance, that it was risky, or that times were hard. If he really wished to produce your work, his brief formula was, "Just draw up a memorandum while I write the cheque."

In the little comedy above mentioned, he played the character of a good-hearted, well-to-do farmer, who is with difficulty roused into a conflict with two of his neighbours by their affronts to his wife. In embodying this part, he displayed his remarkable power of individualization, his genuine feeling, and his happy and varied truthfulness of illustration.

Few actors, indeed, have had a wider range. The heroes of poetic tragedy, or those of high comedy, he scarcely attempted, his Tartuffe being an exception. Probably, however, he was not without ambition to make the trial. On one occasion I read to him a scene or two from an uncompleted serious play in blank verse, of which his estimate was only too generous. "But who," asked he, "is to play the chief character?" "Mr. Benjamin Webster," was the answer, "if he will." He was more touched than the occasion accounted for. "What!" said he, with a warm grasp of the hand; "do you really think I would sustain the chief part, almost tragic, in a poetic drama?" Having expressed my wish that he should make the experiment, he replied,—"I should like it—I should like it, but——" Perhaps there was reason in that "but." His true feeling and his happiness in presenting individual traits in prose drama might not have stood him in such good stead in imaginative work, where the characteristic is rather of that large kind which paints human nature in general, than of that minute kind which paints the peculiarities as well as the passions of individual men. It happened, however, that the drama referred to remained unfinished; thus the test which the actor proposed to himself never was applied. But, even in the sphere of what is called "real life," what variety, and what distinctness of conception, were at Webster's command! To show this it is only necessary to glance at him in a few of his leading embodiments. In 1847 he appeared in " The Roused Lion," taken from a clever French original, " Le Reveil du Lion." Stanislas de Fonblanche, the part which he represented, was that of a man rather advanced in life, and, at the beginning of the piece, somewhat of an invalid. A letter has been received by his godson, in which one of his young and thoughtless acquaintances speaks in contemptuous terms of the elderly gentleman, of the consulate, and the empire, and suggests that, with his obsolete fashions and grave years, he would be a mere kill-joy at a party of pleasure in the days of the Citizen - King. Stanislas Fonblanche, though elderly, is by no means superannuated, and is roused by this reflection upon the manners and accomplishments of a former generation. Accordingly, he contrives to attend a dinner at which his detractor and his godson are to be present. The nature of the entertainment is a little *fête*, and thus admits of sundry exhibitions of talents, such as singing, dancing, and fencing, in the presence of ladies, which are seldom displayed at a dinner-table. The object of Stanislas

Fonblanche is to punish Hector de Mauléon,
by engaging with him in a strife of wits, and
proving his own superiority. This he does
most effectually. If Hector ventures upon a
sarcasm disguised as a compliment, or upon an
affected and overdone politeness, his elderly
rival meets him with a repartee as polite as
it is crushing, and an easy, high-bred courtesy of
the old school, beside which Hector's modern
airs look very much like ill-breeding. In singing, dancing, at cards, with the foils, and in
other ways, he thoroughly conquers and humiliates
him, and becomes, especially to the fairer portion
of the company, the central and captivating
figure. From the easy languor of the invalid
at the beginning, to the high-toned and temperate
triumph at the end, Webster was admirable, not
only in each phase of the character, in each
detail of action, but in the ease and nature which
gave unity and consistency to all his transitions.
I remember the critic of an influential paper, who
was otherwise loud in the comedian's praise,
charging him with a certain want of refinement.

What seemed surprising to me, on the other hand, was the presence of this quality in an actor who had shone hitherto chiefly in rough and strong parts. We are all, perhaps, too much disposed to see in an actor the absence or the lack of qualities which we are accustomed to expect from him. It would be ungrateful to omit from this notice of the "Roused Lion" an allusion to Mrs. Keeley's wonderful rendering of Mademoiselle Suzanne Grasset de Villedieu, formerly a *danseuse*, who is anxious to hide her old vocation from Stanislas, while, in moments of emotion, every look and tone, every gesture of head, feet, and arms, unconsciously betray it.

In May, 1852, Mr. Webster appeared at the Haymarket in a play by Mr. Mark Lemon, entitled, "Mind your Own Business." Though not nominally the hero of the piece, he was such effectually. As a country squire, one Verdon, who has set his affections where they cannot be returned, and who passes from a state of over-sanguine anticipation to one of utter reck-lessness and self-abandonment, he was equally striking, natural, and truthful in each of these contrasting moods. There was now and then a dash of constraint and misgiving in the midst of his hopefulness, which showed the sensitiveness of his disposition and the depth of suffering which the rejection of his love would entail; while in flying to town, in the attempt to drown his misery by gambling and drink, the gleams of a better nature at times broke forth with a pathos all the more affecting because, instead of being sharply contrasted with the darker shades of his character, it was so blended with them as to indicate the same individuality. The yearning of a besotted mind towards a higher life seemed as natural as the right physical movement of the drunkard when, however unsteadily, he staggers towards home. Notwithstanding all the difficulties of the task, he eminently succeeded in making the position of the drunkard thoroughly pathetic, and in so expressing "the soul of goodness in things evil" that they became touching instead of repulsive. But for the strange improbability in the story, which, after

all that Verdon had suffered for love of the one
sister, would persuade us that his affections had
been all the time unconsciously given to the
other, the piece, owing to Webster's acting,
would have been a lasting success.

In his rendering of Verdon, as in other parts,
the two signal merits of the comedian's acting
were comprehensiveness of conception and nice
gradation in the expression of feeling. He knew
that, with rare exceptions, one leading trait seldom
gains such ascendency in a man as not to be
modified by others. I have seen him, for instance, take part in a quarrel-scene, in which a
number of qualities had to be expressed and
harmonised. At the beginning, when sarcasm
and taunts were levelled at him, he responded
by a smile of quiet humour, a shrug of the
shoulders, and a deprecatory movement of the
hands; as the provocation continued, his annoyance was evident, but no less evident the strong
common sense by which he chose to master it.
His look next became fixed and stern, like that
of one who feels a fight inevitable; and when at

length his wife was attacked by cruel sneers, and he suddenly blazed up in indignation, you felt how much his anger had gained in effect from his previous self-control—that the very restraints that had at first checked the flame were now its fuel.

It was, perhaps, his success in "Mind Your Own Business" that led him, in 1855, at the Adelphi, to undertake the tragical representation of another drunkard, Richard Pride, in Mr. Boucicault's drama of "Janet Pride." So powerful in this part was his rendering of the vitiating effects of excess, and of the remorse which struggles with them, that Richard Pride took rank with his most striking impersonations.

As another instance of Webster's versatility, ought to be cited his performance of Graves, in Lord Lytton's comedy of "Money." The conviction that he was born to an unhappy lot, and that the finger of adverse fate went out against him in the smallest trifle, was for a time deep and pervading; and when at last the seductions of Lady Franklin took effect upon him, his change to a sanguine mood was gradual and distrustful;

so that in the dance with Lady Franklin, to
which he at last abandons himself, there was
the quaintest expression in his face of dawning
mirth, mingled with habitual melancholy in his
movements — fantastic and astonished pleasure
so characterized by solemnity, that the novel
humour of the representation was irresistible. I
have seen in other comedians, notably in the
very effective Thomas Thorne, broader contrasts
in the part of Graves, which perhaps elicited
louder laughter; but the Graves of Webster
still remains uppermost in my mind, as a
being who, though somewhat exaggerated by the
author, one might have met in the flesh.

In 1852, in the new piece of "Masks and
Faces," he played one of his finest characters—
that of Triplet, the needy dramatist and portrait
painter, whom, with his family, Peg Woffington
saves from starvation. The study of Triplet in
the actor's hands might be taken as a type of
the penurious author of the time. The distraction
amidst the sordid cares of life; the nervous
impatience, soon atoned for by contrition; the

moods of gloomy reverie, at times half pierced
by the hope of a nature originally sanguine, but
which time and suffering had tamed and daunted;
the desperation with which, when unable to
please himself with Peg's likeness, he plunged
his knife through the canvas, together with an
artlessness of look and voice which spoke an
unworldly mind,—all these degrees of the better
mental worker were so truly indicated, that a
glance, a change of tone, however delicate, a stoop,
a step backward or forward, or a fluttering
movement of the hand, were more significant
even than the excellent dialogue in which he
took part.   And withal this Triplet was a
gentleman; no poverty of garb or surroundings
could hide that; while the perfect unconsciousness
with which this inner refinement showed itself,
was a touch of art so true and unpretending, that
it was seen only in its effects.

The Peg Woffington of Mrs. Stirling, it may
be added, was one of the best, probably *the* best,
of her original characters.

Towards the end of 1846 Webster was the hero

of "The Round of Wrong," a drama by Bayle
Bernard, which, though well-written and con-
taining some good situations, was elaborate to
heaviness, and thus narrowly missed popularity.
The acting of the principal character was, however, so fine as to deserve record. In Reuben
Gwynne, engaged to marry a girl who afterwards
sadly rejects him at the instigation of her father,
no changes of character could be more complete,
and at the same time more consistent, than those
which the actor depicted. The honest cheerfulness, the good-natured liberality of the happy
lover who would spread the joy he feels, were
shown to the life, as were also the bitterness,
the avarice, and the vindictiveness of the man
whose hopes and whose faith had been trodden
down. Yet, in both aspects, Reuben Gwynne
was seen to be the same man. His misanthropy
was the reaction against his loving credulity.
His longing for vengeance was the wild outcome
of his suffering—the mad desire to give torture
vent which makes the wounded creature turn
upon the hunter. When at length the tables

were turned, and his enemy, the father of his
old love, lay at his mercy, nothing could be truer
than the manner—most gradual in its rise, but
sudden in its end—in which the cherished purpose of revenge gradually yielded before the
prayers and influence of his restored darling.
The spring of his life had returned; the ice
which had concealed it for a while broke, and
there was the living current.

Another celebrated character of this actor
was that of Tartuffe, in a version by Mr.
Oxenford, originally produced at the Haymarket.
He had here to pass from the embodiment of
strong or fierce passions, emotions of hearty
good-nature and honest anger, of grief and
remorse, ōr of tender emotions, threaded by
quaint and simple humours, to that of dissimulation, which is, at all events, meant to be as
profound as it is unscrupulous. It may be
heresy in the writer to take a strong exception
to what some regard as Molière's *chef-d'œuvre*,
but he has striven in vain to think that
the hypocrisy of Tartuffe is, on the whole,

subtle and plausible. It has always seemed to him, on the contrary, to be so overdone as to advertise unmistakably its own imposture. It was one of Mr. Webster's great merits in the part, that he moderated its excesses as far as he could, and brought it as near to a human possibility as his actions would enable him. The assumption was entirely successful, and Tartuffe became one of Webster's stock parts; thus furnishing one more proof of his power to translate himself with equal effect into the most opposite characters. That of a Jesuit priest, which he played at the Adelphi, in Mr. Charles Reade's "Two Loves and a Life," was a striking, though far less elaborate picture of a higher kind of cleric, in whom the restraint of a strong will upon strong passions was admirably exemplified.

As an expression of power, however, nothing short of tragic must be cited his rendering of Robert Landry, in the first act of the Adelphi drama, "The Dead Heart." Landry, a young sculptor, by the machinations of a certain Count de St. Valerie and a godless priest, is immured

on false pretexts in the Bastille. The object of
St. Valerie in the vile proceeding is to bring
within his snare a lovely and innocent girl
betrothed to Landry. Nearly twenty years after
this shameful deed comes the taking of the
Bastille by the infuriated masses, the murder of
the defenders, and the release of the prisoners.
Of these last Landry is one. But the long-
immured man, crushed by despair, solitude, and
the rigour of his treatment, seems to have lost
alike consciousness and sensation. The ghastly
face, the long and matted hair, the rigid limbs,
seem at first to speak of mere inert matter. It
is, however, matter faintly stirred with breath
that is brought back to day. All means of
restoration are employed, but vainly, till the
urgent repetition of a name—that of his betrothed
—draws forth a tremulous response, after which
the gradual resuscitation of bodily and mental
life sets in. But the conduct of the process was
a masterpiece of art. At first Landry lay like
a fossil. It was as if different forces of nature
passed one into another—mineral existence

thawing into the mobility of animal life, animal life groping its way into human consciousness, and irritating it from its apathy, till at last one saw the recovered man in the forlorn dignity of his memory and his wrongs. No scene capable of such great treatment by the actor occurs in the remainder of the drama. This one scene, however, can hardly be forgotten by those who saw it. Mr. Webster, however, was fine throughout the piece. Let me record here how admirable I thought Mr. David Fisher's representation in this play of the unscrupulous and disdainful *abbé*, whose hateful and malignant nature is rendered just bearable by his scorn of danger. Having seen Mr. Fisher in several parts which he filled like a true artist, I have often wondered that he was not more frequently before the town in important characters.

It was not my good fortune to see Mr. Webster in a small piece, in which he was, by general consent, allowed to be at his best. As the poor dramatic copyist, Penn Holder, in " One Touch of Nature," he had a part which gave scope to all his yearning tenderness as a father, and to restraints scarcely less touching, by which he, for a time, was forced to check it. He had to make himself known to a daughter who had no recollection of him, at so early an age had she been carried off by the guilty mother who deserted her husband. The daughter, under the name of Constance Belmour, was then an actress. A private rehearsal takes place in the house of a dramatic author, who is dissatisfied with Constance, in the stage-fiction, for her coldness when she has to recognize a father who holds a position precisely analogous to that of Holder to Constance. Fearful that his daughter should lose the chance of acting the part, Holder proposes in this rehearsal to take the character of the supposed father, and, in doing so, relates a number of real details which gradually bring back to the girl's dormant memory her first home and the indistinct vision of a loving father. In brief, Constance throws herself into the old man's arms, and learns from her new experience of filial love how to sustain her part of daughter in the drama.

It should be added, that while Holder has been striving to reawaken her memory as a stage-father, he has been trembling lest he should reveal his true character too soon, and that, in portraying these alternations of fond impulsiveness and needful self-suppression, Webster gained a triumph that he had scarcely surpassed. From the slight sketch given of Penn Holder's character, I can well believe his excellence in it.

This sterling actor had few faults; perhaps among the chief of them was a certain heaviness and sombreness in playing the young heroes of comedy. Thus his Petrucchio seemed really violent and angry, and showed little enjoyment of the part in which he was masquerading. His Wildrake, too, in "The Love-Chase," was over-sullen and moody. These parts wanted the geniality and the touches of humour with which he so often relieved his older characters, and even his young ones, when they were *au fond* rather grave than gay. In his later years, too, whether from carelessness or too much occupation, he was seldom perfect in the text when he appeared

in a new part. A "fishing for words" and
dragging delivery took away from his effects,
till he warmed into his part, recovered his
memory, or supplied the loss of it impromptu.
He took leave of the stage in 1874. From the
farewell benefit accorded to him at Drury Lane
the same year, few indeed of his more distinguished brothers and sisters in art were absent.
He had truly deserved well of his profession.
His services as a manager rivalled those he had
rendered as an actor. He had assembled a
company of actors so numerous, as well as
brilliant, that the accidental absence of one star
could at once be substituted by another. He
had sought to bring to light new dramatic ability
by offers which, if they now seem moderate,
were then liberality itself, and in the course of
his sixteen years' management, it is said, had
paid thirty thousand pounds to his authors. It
was rumoured that in later years, at the Adelphi,
his outlay was less generous. If true that he had
learnt, from hard experience, to be thrifty, it is
scarcely to be wondered at.

Amongst other plays of the writer, he produced, at the Haymarket, in 1847, a comedy
entitled "The Heart and the World." It was a
piece of so purely a psychological nature as to
neglect incident, which, instead of being presented with fulness and strength, was only so
far outlined as to give a key to mental conditions. This unsuccessful piece is mentioned
only to show how lightly at that time the
manager bore pecuniary failure. He had built
great hopes on the piece, the reception of which
on the first night was cold, though not hostile.
That its "run" was doubtful was an impression
which its author had at once formed, and which
he took no especial pains to hide from the
cordial manager, who accompanied him home to
a little social gathering, and did his best to cheer
him on the way. "We shall make a stand," he
said. "In a night or two all will have warmed
to their work, and the piece will go twice as
briskly." When, however, the notices of the new
play had appeared, and even the kindest of them
did not predict its attraction, it was felt that

the general opinion could not be resisted.
Without a murmur at his own loss or disappointment, Mr. Webster did all he could to put
the baffled dramatist in heart, spoke of his
unshaken faith in him, of successes that were
soon to sponge out the present failure, and
showed himself indeed the staunch friend that
he has already been described.

Not very long before the memorable Shakspere
Tercentenary, 1863, a dinner was given to
Webster at the Freemasons' Tavern. The unfortunate Shakspere Committee was at that time
seeking to raise funds for a memorial of the
poet. It was curious to hear the guest of the
evening demand, almost in terms of menace, that,
in honour of Shakspere, a large part of the sums
raised should be awarded to the two establish-
ments of which he was founder—the Dramatic
and Equestrian Institution, and the Home for
Decayed Actors at Woking. There was good
reason that these undertakings should be supported by contemporary generosity, but very
little that they should divert from its course

the money raised for a personal tribute, the best form of which would obviously have been a statue. Webster's interest, however, in institutions which he had founded, magnified to him their claims, and led him to urge them even with excessive warmth. Very agreeable, however, are the recollections of that night at the Freemasons'. Webster was full of reminiscences of old times and of brother-actors. He spoke, too, with much satisfaction of the cordial reception given him in Paris by Napoleon the Third, whom he had formerly known in London. Robert Bell, our genial and eloquent chairman, proposed the guest's health in a speech full of criticism and felicitous expression. The formalities of the evening then gave way to pleasant gossip, jest, and repartee. At a rather late hour came in Mr. Robert Keeley, who had some time before retired from the stage, and whose entrance was the signal for a burst of welcome, and for one more toast, tumultuously received. Webster was now at the height of his reputation. A few years later his appearance became gradually rarer and rarer. He survived his farewell of the stage more than eight years. He died in the summer of 1882, at the age of eighty-four, leaving as a realistic actor a reputation hardly surpassed for force, pathos, and humour, conveyed by incisive and subtle detail; leaving, as a man, the memory of an influential and honourable career of liberality in his engagements, and of loyalty in his friendships.

CHAPTER IX.

MRS. GLOVER.

Mrs. Glover in e rly days had often appeared in tragedy—Had
performed E mlet—First saw her as Gertrude, to Charles
Kemble's Hamlet—Her eminence as an actress of comedy—
Her truth to nature—Her keen perception of characteristics,
moderation, and air of unconsciousness—These merits
exemplified in her Mrs. Malaprop—Her performance of
the character compared with Mrs. Stirling's—Mrs. Glover's
Mrs. Candour—Her Nurse in "Romeo and Juliet"—Her
Widow Green in "The Love Chase"—The original Lady
Franklin in "Money"—Her Miss Tucker in "Time
Works Wonders"—She appears in a comedy called "The
Maiden Aunt," by R. B. Knowles—Acts in the writer's
comedy, "Borough Politics"—Account of her performance
—Meeting with her at rehearsal—An argument with the
author—Minuteness and fulness of her observation—
Her sympathy with authors—Thackeray's tribute to her
acting—Reported connection of her family with the famous
Betterton—Her death.

In early life Mrs. Glover had often performed
tragic parts, Hamlet amongst the rest. The
character in which I first saw her was Gertrude
in " Hamlet."   I was too much absorbed in Charles

Kemble's acting to give her the attention that
was her due, but I well recall her aspect of settled
melancholy and the sad, deep tones of her voice.
Tragedy, however, was become with her, in
general, a thing of the past. She had then given
up youthful characters, but, as an actress of
comedy in her own line, as the Nurse in " Romeo
and Juliet," as Mrs. Heidelberg, Mrs. Malaprop,
Mrs. Candour, and as Widow Green in " The
Love Chase," she was without an equal.

In reviewing a number of performers whose
merits are often alike in everything but degree,
it becomes difficult to apply epithets which have
not lost something of their force by repetition.
To say simply that Mrs. Glover's main excellence
was her truth to nature, though no doubt literally
correct, would hardly tell anything. Edmund
Kean, for instance, Macready, the Kembles, were,
of course, generally true to the passions and
characters they represented. But this truthfulness can only be general in tragedy which represents the essential feelings men have in
common, and rejects everything that savours

of mere peculiarity. In comedy, however, which represents the idiosyncrasies of persons, and the modes in which men differ, the expression of vivid personality is often one of the highest merits. This Mrs. Glover eminently possessed. She had an instinct for seizing traits and humours, a moderation in displaying them as just as her perception of them was lively, a wide range of appreciation, and an apparent unconsciousness which gave wonderful reality to her delineations. Thus, in the eccentricities of her parts of speech as Mrs. Malaprop, and in her displays of vanity and credulity, there was a solemn self-complacency, an absence of misgiving, an obtuseness to ridicule, a *vis inertiæ* of comedy, so to speak, which, in its power to produce the ludicrous, could not have been surpassed by the most active exertions. Those who, having seen Mrs. Glover in Mrs. Malaprop, have also seen Mrs. Stirling's admirably telling delineation, full of intrigue, life, and movement, of the same part, have had an opportunity of seeing the utmost that two differing methods can produce, and of

comparing their effects. In the hands of each,
the general outlines of a character so broadly
defined as Mrs. Malaprop were, of course,
identical. The difference—and it was considerable—lay in shades of expression. In uttering
the grandiloquent phraseology of the part, Mrs.
Glover's self-satisfaction was more restrained, but
not less profound, than Mrs. Stirling's. The
former seemed to hug the secret of her superiority, the latter to revel in its presumed effect
upon her listeners. The compliments of Captain
Absolute were received by Mrs. Glover with
evident pleasure, indeed, but with a consciousness
that they were absolutely her due; by Mrs.
Stirling with a flutter of delighted vanity. In
hearing herself described as " an old weather-
beaten she-dragon," resentment predominates with
Mrs. Stirling, whilst with Mrs. Glover an appealing astonishment against the profanity of the
impeachment was the leading sentiment. There
are now few who have had a chance of contrasting the claims of these two admirable
actresses in the part in question; but even those

who have the liveliest recollection of Mrs. Glover
will recognize in Mrs. Stirling's Mrs. Malaprop
the finest example of old comedy acting left to
the contemporary stage.

In Mrs. Candour, again, Mrs. Glover, when
uttering her charitable calumnies, wore an air
of almost deep and stolid conviction, which
showed that the hypocrite, imposing even upon
herself, believed that she was defending her
victims while she enjoyed the pleasure of traducing.
them.

Her Nurse in "Romeo and Juliet" had all
the reality of Dutch art applied to character.
Her attachment to her youthful charge was
strong even to audacity. Her remonstrance with
old Capulet, when he threatens and abuses Juliet
for refusing the proposed marriage with Paris,
had a sullen, half-checked fierceness in it, like
the growl of an angry but wary dog when one
attacks his mistress. Her attachment to Juliet
was, indeed, a sort of animal instinct. It exerted
no general influence; it helped to humour, but
not to understand or fathom, the young girl's

love. She wore a look of puzzled indulgence when listening to Juliet's grief for Romeo's banishment. For a while this, with the Nurse, was a whim to be humoured, by no means to be persisted in at the risk of loss or danger. In all this, of course, the actress only followed Shakspere; but her manner of doing so was perfect. If self-interest had been an article of the Decalogue, she could not have obeyed it with more implicit faith, with more utter unconsciousness of its meanness. There was a sort of frank rationality in her mien and manner when she urged Juliet to desert her lover, as of one who spoke from her deepest convictions. Her very conscience seemed to be dishonest.

Of her performance of such characters as we have already named, including Mrs. Heidelberg in the "Clandestine Marriage," criticism has taken more ample note than of her acting in more modern plays—of her "Widow Green," for instance, in Sheridan Knowles's "Love Chase." This, however, was one of her best characters. What a complacent confidence was there in her

mature charms, when she questions her maid as
to the signs of young Master Walter's disappointment at her absence; what enjoyment of
her supposed lover's mortification, what eagerness in her desire to repair it; what indignant
disdain for Lydia's pure and disinterested conception of love; what elation at the power of
her own attractions, where Master Walter's letter,
with the offer of marriage to her maid, falls by
mistake into her hands; what truth to nature
when it strikes the buxom widow that she looks
too saucily happy for the timid bride she fain
would personate—

> "Amelia, give this feather more a slope
> That it sit droopingly.
> *   *   *   *   *
> Hang this cheek
> Of mine! it is too saucy. What a pity
> To have a colour of one's own!"

And then, how fine and natural were the gradations from rage at her self-deception touching
Master Walter to the politic conclusion that, being
dressed for the altar, she would do well to escape
ridicule by marrying the elderly Sir William
Fondlove. Selfish, vain, cunning, worldly, but,

on the whole, good-humoured, and with a pleasure in herself that made her pleasant to others, the actress presented a character, the traits of which might easily have been spoiled by exaggeration, with a force which was increased by her moderation—a moderation, be it understood, in which there was nothing tame—and with a harmonious variety which, after a night's acquaintance, made one feel as if one had known Widow Green all one's life.

In 1840, during Mr. Webster's management of the Haymarket, Mrs. Glover, was the original Lady Franklin in Lord Lytton's comedy of "Money." Here, for once, it was possible to take exception to her. She wanted the due enjoyment of her intrigue and the vivacity needed to captivate a nature like that of Graves. She was also, in 1840, the Miss Tucker of Douglas Jerrold's comedy of "Time Works Wonders." As the punctilious schoolmistress, she gave lively and amusing expression to the peculiarities of the part; but the comedy was so crowded with figures that she had relatively little opportunity to do so. At the Haymarket also, while with Mr. Webster, she played the part of the Maiden Aunt in the comedy of that name by Mr. R. B. Knowles, son of the celebrated dramatist. Her delightful geniality and spirit in this character was the mainstay of the piece, which, though slight in plot, had for a *coup d'essai* considerable merit. I am not aware, however, that Mr. R. B. Knowles made any second dramatic attempt.

In 1846 I had the pleasure of securing Mrs. Glover's services for a two-act comedy of my own, entitled "Borough Politics." I had thus an opportunity of observing, at rehearsal, how thoroughly she had entered into her part, omitting no opportunity of watching her relations to the other characters in the piece, or their modifying influence upon herself, the good-hearted but uneducated woman married to a worthy farmer, with a daughter betrothed to the son of supercilious neighbours. The chief trial of Mrs. Thompson (Mrs. Glover's part), at the opening of the piece, is the contempt with

which Dr. and Mrs. Neville regard her efforts
to rise in the social scale. The ostentatious re-
furnishing of Mrs. Thompson's house has given
Mrs. Neville an opportunity for exhausting her
powers of sarcasm on the former, who, incensed
by a long series of affronts, invokes her husband's
protection. Upon this Nathan Thompson, the
husband, resolves to dispute in his own person
Dr. Neville's election to the mayoralty—a resolution which has the unhappy effect of separating
the two lovers of the piece, each of whom now
belongs to a rival house. It will be assumed
that this sterling actress brought out with
admirable effect the delight of the worthy
matron in self-display, in the overdone splendour
of her residence, her sullen attempts to conceal
her mortification under the civil contempt of
Mrs. Neville, and the overflow of genuine passion
with which she at last retorted upon her, exulting
in the success of every well-delivered blow.
Nor was her maternal grief less effective, when,
her anger fading, she felt that she had brought
about a separation between her daughter and her

daughter's suitor, and converted her apparently easy-going husband into a man stern and vindictive and a great stickler for ceremonies. All this may be affirmed, and yet it will not show the special point in which Mrs. Glover differed from many capable actresses — that absorption in her part which no mere clever-ness of delivery, however appropriate, can sub-stitute or imitate. Take one illustration. When her husband, as probable mayor, is spoken of as "his worship," the title sinks deeply into the mind of his wife. Though she had nothing immediately to say, her expression showed that she was rolling it over like a sweet morsel. Knowing that in some cases the rank of the husband gives a new appellation to the wife— that the spouse of a lord or baronet, for instance, becomes "lady"—poor Mrs. Thompson is anxious to know how she will be styled as the wife of "his worship." Over this question Mrs. Glover fondly brooded, till she sadly discovered that the honorary phrase of "worship" given to a mayor still left his wife a simple "Mrs." The con-

versation then turned on other points. She now
and then gave a languid attention to it, and
then relapsed into her reverie, illustrated by her
dejected looks and restless movements. When
she at length rose, with the exclamation, "It's
hard, though, there aren't no female 'worship!'"
she produced a burst of laughter, by disclosing
to the audience in words the trouble which,
with so much quiet nature, she had expressed
in pantomime.

At rehearsal, during the feigned anger of the
farmer-squire at his daughter's melancholy, Mrs.
Glover made an expressive gesture indicating
that all was right between the two. I thought
this rather premature, and observed that the
father had said nothing to justify it. She pointed
out to me, however, that, according to the stage
direction, the mention of his daughter had already
cost him a display of emotion. "Oh," said she,
"don't you think that if such a father is once
moved by the thought of his child, she's sure
to carry the day? It was because I saw him
struggling with his feelings that I put on that

look of pleasure. I felt convinced, at least for
the moment, that he would forgive her." The
author deferred to an argument which showed
that the actress had more closely studied one
of his characters than he had done. He would
apologize for dwelling on this little drama,
were it not that his presence at rehearsal gave
him an opportunity of noticing the minuteness
and fulness of Mrs. Glover's observation more
closely than he could have done from her acting.
The effects of these qualities might have been
equally felt "at night," but the intellectual
subtlety of motive that led to them would have
been partly missed. On the day after the production of the little piece, it happened that
one journal spoke less favourably of it than
the general press. I remarked to Mrs. Glover
that the criticism in question nevertheless paid
the warmest possible tribute to herself. "Oh,
that may be," said the actress, with all the
warmth and sincerity which look and tone can
convey; "but I never feel happy unless the
author has his full share of praise with us."

After the piece had been performed a few nights, I had the pleasure of meeting Thackeray, who expressed the warmest admiration of Mrs. Glover's acting in it.

It has been asserted that Mrs. Glover, whose maiden name was Betterton, inherited the blood of the famous actor who flourished in the reign of Charles the Second, and his successors. If the assertion be true, the right to such honourable descent was well maintained by this excellent actress. She died in 1850, at the age of sixty-eight.

CHAPTER X.

Mrs. Warner's rank as an actress—Performs both the gentler
and sterner characters in tragedy—At Covent Garden
and Drury Lane with Macready—Had appeared, in 1836,
as the heroine of Knowles's "Daughter"—Her Joan of
Arc, Lady Macbeth, and Hermione—Her power in invective and in irony—Her fine impersonations of Emilia in
"Othello," and of Evadne in "The Maid's Tragedy"—
Account of her acting in these characters—Evadne her
chief triumph—Enthusiastic praise of it by Dickens—
After separating from Phelps, Mrs. Warner attempts, in
1847, to make the Marylebone Theatre a Western Sadler's
Wells—Eventual failure of the scheme—During her
management of the Marylebone, Mrs. Warner appears
as Hermione, Julia, Lady Teazle, Mrs. Beverley, Mrs.
Oakley, and Lady Townley—Her want of flexibility in
comedy—Great merit, nevertheless, of her Mrs. Oakley—
The event of her first season at the Marylebone the
magnificent and correct reproduction of Beaumont and
Fletcher's "Scornful Lady"—Remarks on this Comedy—
The character of the heroine remarkably suited to her—
Mrs. Warner in private—First meeting with her at
rehearsal at Drury Lane, in 1842—Her acute and
humorous remarks on Macready's realistic getting up
of "The Patrician's Daughter"—Anecdote told by her of

impracticable stage-effects—Her easy and genial manners
in private, for the exhibition of which her stage characters
gave few opportunities—Her last illness and death.

MRS. WARNER was a remarkable actress, even at
the time when Miss Helen Faucit and Mrs.
Charles Kean were at the height of their popularity. In serious characters she was second only
to them in public estimation, playing, moreover,
a range of sterner characters than they generally
appeared in. At the time of her engagements
with Macready, both at Covent Garden and at
Drury Lane, Miss Huddart, who, in the course of
them, became Mrs. Warner, was the recognized
Lady Macbeth, Emilia, Gertrude, and Volumnia
of those theatres. In 1836 she had made a
considerable impression in a part of a strong,
but more amiable description—the heroine of
Knowles's "Daughter," a play which, though
gloomy, might for pure dramatic force compete
with any of his productions. I did not see Mrs.
Warner (then Miss Huddart) in the character
mentioned; but it is due to her to record the
warm approval which she received from press

and public in a more winning part than those she usually represented.

It may be mentioned here that, in 1837, at Covent Garden, she personated the heroine of a melodrama called "Joan of Arc," the critics generally deposing to her energy and intensity, though one or two accused her, not quite unjustly, of occasional ranting.

Lady Macbeth, though probably the character which Mrs. Warner most frequently impersonated, was not, in my opinion, her most successful one. It had a tolerably well counterfeited air of the true personage, but it would not stand the tests of long acquaintanceship or examination. In the early acts, it was stern, set, decisive, and when need was, impetuous and scornful; but there was all the difference between it and a genuine conception that exists between a character arrived at and expressed by the understanding, and a character seized by the will and inspired with its energy. There was not that variety of tone or manner which belongs to a woman desperately bent upon an end, and eager to try every resource in turn to secure it. There was a declamatory attempt in the first scene to realize the supernatural, but no real awe, no real trust in "fate" and "metaphysical aid." In the later scenes, Mrs. Warner was dignified and remorseful, and the solemnities of the sleep-walking scene were punctiliously observed, and rendered with all the time-honoured traditions. What, then, did she lack? Depth, incisiveness, the interchange of the shifting moods of emotion, the different shades even of the same emotion which mark life. Yet there was, so to speak, such a consistent *physique* of Lady Macbeth in Mrs. Warner's delineation, and such a propriety in her somewhat surface-exhibition of the character, that she was held for years to be its most satisfactory representative.

Among the few gentler types of womanhood that she occasionally embodied, was Hermione in the "Winter's Tale." She gave with great dignity and queenly patience that wonderful defence of the slandered queen, in which the story of her wrong gains emphasis and force from

its moderation. Nothing could be more royal
than her appearance in the statue-scene, more
finely graduated than the return to life and
motion, or more nobly affecting than her final
embrace of the repentant Leontes.

She had great power in direct invective, as
well as in irony. In the latter she sometimes
employed a sinister gentleness, which implied
far more scorn than open bitterness could
compass. Her Emilia in "Othello" was finely
conceived and executed. She showed a bold
freedom of manner, which went far to justify
Iago's suspicions of her. With this was combined that sort of half *blasé* ease which comes
from knowledge of life, however gained, and of
the chief figures of the time, while the whole
was lit up and half redeemed by the sudden
flashes of that more generous spirit by which
Shakspere has hinted what the wife of Iago
might have been under better conditions. Her
usual characteristic was breadth rather than
subtlety, except in pride, of which she had all
the *nuances*. It might be going too far to

ascribe her devotion to Desdemona to some remorseful tenderness for one who was the image
of her past and purer life. Nevertheless, her
acting perfectly tallied with such a conception.
She was a different, and, on the whole, a higher
being with Desdemona than with others. After
the murder of Desdemona, her defiance to Othello
when she rates him, " I care not for thy sword,"
had the passionate recklessness of life which
indignation creates, and her entire acting in the
passages where she discloses the villainy of her
husband was fraught with a fierce anguish of
bereavement for her mistress, as well as scorn for
her husband and his dupe.   For better, for worse,
she was that marvellous embodiment of a nature
grown unscrupulous through its fall, and yet
morally clear-sighted, and capable of generosity
and attachment, that Shakspere has painted
with a success equal to his daring.

There can be no doubt, however, that Mrs.
Warner won her chief triumph as Evadne in
" The Bridal "—Sheridan Knowles's adaptation of
" The Maid's Tragedy," first played at the Hay-

market, in 1837. Scorn never took a more regal
mien, guilt never borrowed a more redeeming
touch of majesty from resolution, self-possession,
and contempt of look and tone—all the more
withering because they were kept within the
bounds of calm restraint, as if Evadne would not
allow herself to be much moved by so slight a
cause as this new convenience, this despised
husband. Her first careless disregard of his ex-
postulation, followed by the cold gaze of her
lustrous eyes on him, when he forced her to be
explicit, made an admirable contrast. There is
a passage in which she asks him what look of
hers suits him best. Amintor replies—

> "Why do you ask?
> *Evad.* That I may show you one less pleasing to you.
> *Amin.* How's that?
> *Evad.* That I may show you one less pleasing to you.

In the repetition of this answer, her tones
were so clear and slow that each syllable took
its fullest meaning, and carried home to Amintor
the conviction of her recoil from him. When,
subsequently, she warns him that it is no
maiden coyness that bids her shrink from his

arms; that "hot and rising blood" makes her
apt indeed for love, but that her beauty pledged
to the king shall not stoop to any second wooer,
there was an exaltation in the avowal of her
guilty passion for her paramour which made
her seem an embodiment of sensual beauty,
inspired by passion and ignorant of conscience.
If I mistake not, it was in this scene that she
wore a large necklace of pearls, which threw
the haughty, and, if I may use such an epithet,
the sultry splendour of her face into grand relief.

This scene with Amintor was, indeed, a brilliant
passage. Nowise inferior to it was her interview
with Melantius, when, having discovered her
dishonour, he extorts from her a confession as to
her betrayer. Her levity and prompt resource
of equivocation while she yet doubts her brother's
meaning, her haughty and imperious defiance
when she at length apprehends it, disclosing a
strain of resolution akin to his own, her submission only at the last extremity, when he has
wrought upon her shame as well as her terror,
were painted to the height, while the praise of

a fine artist was due for her skill in softening Evadne's abrupt change from defiance to repentance.

Not long after the revival of "The Bridal," I met Charles Dickens at dinner at the Clarendon Hotel.* In the course of the evening we spoke together of the acting of Macready and Mrs. Warner in this play. "What a defiant, splendid Sin that woman is!" exclaimed Dickens, with enthusiasm. "How superbly, too, she looks the part!" In short, the great novelist did not speak with more delight of his friend Macready in Melantius (one of his signal triumphs), than of Mrs. Warner in Evadne.

After separating from Mr. Phelps, Mrs. Warner opened, in 1847, the Marylebone Theatre, probably hoping to gain a western suburb the same reputation for legitimacy which had followed the

---

* This dinner was given in honour of the benevolent Dr. Southwood Smith, the late Lord Lansdowne occupying the chair. In a book of theatrical recollections, it may not be out of place to record that the genial Lord Carlisle, better remembered, perhaps, as Lord Morpeth, was one of the company, whom he highly amused by humorously avowing his remarkable likeness to Liston, the comedian.

experiment at Sadler's Wells. In this expecta-
tion, however, after a brave struggle, she was
disappointed. The company by which she was
supported, though respectable, was not equal to
that collected by Phelps at the Islington Theatre.
At the Marylebone, being her own mistress,
Mrs. Warner naturally gave her ambition rather
a wide scope. She opened with her admirable
Hermione in the "Winter's Tale," then played
Julia in "The Hunchback," Lady Teazle in "The
School for Scandal," Mrs. Beverley in "The
Gamester," Mrs. Oakley in "The Jealous Wife,"
Lady Townley in "The Provoked Husband,"
securing for all the characters least suited for
her that measure of acceptance which a practised
and intelligent performer can always command.

She was generally somewhat deficient in the
flexibility necessary for the heroines of comedy,
and, indeed, for those heroines whose graver
qualities are relieved by vivacity and humour.
In Mrs. Oakley, however, she displayed remarkable spirit, and that character was probably the
best of her assumptions in purely prose comedy.

But the great event of her first season at the
Marylebone was undoubtedly the revival of
Beaumont and Fletcher's "Scornful Lady,"
through an adaptation furnished by Mr. J. D.
Serle, an actor and dramatist who at that time
had some reputation in both capacities. The
comedy was put upon the stage with a sumptuous
taste and correctness which Macready himself
as a manager could not have exceeded. An
imposing hall and grand staircase, a noble
gallery, running the length of the stage, with
the various apartments from it, and an apartment in the "Lady's house," with its lofty marble
mantelpiece, its various decorations and elegant
trifles all in keeping with the time, were amongst
the chief triumphs of the scenery, while every
costume had been made a careful study. Nothing
could have been more stately than this frame
for Beaumont and Fletcher's picture. It is
doubtful whether the comedy itself quite deserved all the praises for wit and spirit which
were ascribed to it. In other works of these
authors, both these qualities, it seems to the

writer, have been more fully exhibited—a circumstance which is perhaps accounted for by the small share which Fletcher is supposed to have taken in the play. Nevertheless, there is enough of invention, of decisive handling of character and breadth of contrast in the characters to leave it effective, even when purged from some of its grossness. The delineation of the Scornful Lady was one of Mrs. Warner's greatest successes. Her haughty severity, kept within the limits of refined courtesy, well became her, and had a sort of provoking attractiveness both for the public and the ill-used lover.

Though it was Mrs. Warner's lot to appear generally in characters of severity, pride, decision, or, in rarer cases, of stately sorrow, she was, in private, full of *bonhomie*, animation, and quick perception. I first met her at rehearsal, in 1842, on the stage of Drury Lane Theatre. The play in preparation, though in blank verse, was one of contemporary life. Macready was anxious—perhaps more anxious than the author—to invest the action with every detail of the most modern

realism. For this purpose, the season represented
being summer, during one of the acts he wished
the actresses engaged to use parasols. "Blank
verse and parasols," said Mrs. Warner, apart, to
me one morning. "Is not that quite a new
combination?" "Yes," was the answer; "the
wish is to show that the present time has its
poetical aspect." "And you demonstrate that,"
she asked archly, "by carrying parasols, and
insisting upon other little realisms of the time?"
To this, rejoinder was made that the attempt was
to show the poetry of the age, in spite of its
realistic details, and, therefore, they had to be
encountered; and that, inasmuch as it was quite
possible for a woman to feel a poetical sentiment
—love or admiration, for instance—while using
a parasol, it was quite right to allow her to
express the sentiment with such an appendage;
that the seeming incongruity she referred to
sprang from mere novelty of association, and
that it would disappear as the association became
familiar. "But how far will you insist on this
view?" she asked. "If you concede to realism

the uttering of poetical sentiment under parasols, realism will soon demand more, and exact from you that the parasols shall cast their shadows on the ground, and just in accordance with the position of the sun." This, doubtless, seemed to her (for the stage resources of limelight were then little known) a difficulty that could scarcely be overcome. However, the quickness of her observation and her power of deduction were amply shown by her objections, no less than was her vein of pleasant humour in the mode of expressing them.

Shortly after undertaking the management of the Marylebone Theatre, she called on us one morning, and amused us all greatly by anecdotes of the impracticable stage-effects which had been sent to her for representation. One of the dramas she mentioned was founded on a Grecian subject, and required that the defeated hero of the piece, after having been pierced by a javelin, taking advantage probably of the courtesy of his enemies, should ascend the slope of a mountain, and compose himself to die in such an attitude that the rays of the declining sun would just rest upon his brow.*   I give this little anecdote to the best of my memory in Mrs. Warner's own words, though I cannot reproduce the pleasant and easy humour of her expression—all the more noticeable, because she had so few opportunities of exhibiting this quality on the stage.   After much suffering, during which the gracious sympathy of Her Majesty was habitually shown to her, Mrs. Warner died at the age of fifty, in 1854.

* This difficulty, which seemed at the time insurmountable, might now easily be conquered by the employment of limelight.

END OF VOL. I.

LONDON : PRINTED BY WILLIAM CLOWES AND SONS, LIMITED, STAMFORD STREET AND CHARING CROSS.

For EU product safety concerns, contact us at Calle de José Abascal, 56–1°,
28003 Madrid, Spain or eugpsr@cambridge.org.

www.ingramcontent.com/pod-product-compliance
Ingram Content Group UK Ltd.
Pitfield, Milton Keynes, MK11 3LW, UK
UKHW010348140625
459647UK00010B/926